NEW IRISH WALK GUIDES

Southwest

Sean O Suilleabhain

GENERAL EDITOR
JOSS LYNAM

Gill and Macmillan

Published in Ireland by
Gill and Macmillan Ltd
Goldenbridge
Dublin 8
with associated companies throughout the world
© Seán Ó Suilleabháin 1991
Maps drawn by Justin May
0 7171 1795 2
Print origination by
Seton Music Graphics Ltd, Bantry, Co. Cork
Printed by ColourBooks Ltd, Dublin

Based on the Ordnance Survey by
permission of the Government
(Permit No. 5429)

For Rory, Darragh, Orlaith and Ciara

CONTENTS

MOUNTAIN SAFETY

The Irish hills are still relatively unfrequented. This is a happy situation for hill walkers unless they get into serious trouble and needs help. As this may well have to come from a consider-able distance, it is particularly important to take all reasonable precautions.

1. Wear suitable clothing, and regardless of the weather carry extra warm clothes, wind- and water-proof anorak and overtrousers. Except on short, easy walks it is best to wear walking boots.

2. Plan your walk carefully and be sure you can complete it before dark. To estimate walking times, see page 3.

3. Check weather forecasts and keep a look out for weather changes. On high ground mist and rain can close in with alarming speed.

4. Remember that the temperature drops 2–3°C for each 300m/1,000ft you climb and if, as is frequently the case, there is a strong wind the temperature drop will be even more marked. It may be a pleasant day at sea level whilst freezing and windy at 800m/2,500ft.

5. Always carry a map and compass, and learn to use them efficiently in good weather so you will have confidence in your ability to use them in bad. A torch, whistle and small first aid kit should also be taken — remember that the mountain distress signal is six blasts per minute and then a pause.

6. Carry a reserve supply of food including chocolate, glucose tablets, etc., and something warm to drink.

7. Leave word at your hotel, guest house or hostel where you are going, what your route will be and when you intend to get back. If you are parking a car at the beginning of a walk, you can leave a note on the seat.

8. Streams in flood are dangerous and extreme caution is necessary.

9. If your party does have an accident, telephone 999 and ask for Mountain Rescue or contact the local Garda Station who will organise the rescue.

10. Never walk solo, except in areas where there are other people around.

11. Remember that most accidents happen on the descent, when you are tired, so take especial care then.

Some of the precautions listed above are obviously designed for the longer, higher walks but do remember that especially in winter, the Irish hills can be dangerous.

The Country Code

- GUARD AGAINST FIRE. Every year carelessness costs thousands of pounds.
- FASTEN ALL GATES. Animals will wander if they can.
- KEEP DOGS UNDER CONTROL. They should be on a lead wherever there is livestock.

- KEEP TO PATHS ACROSS FARMLAND.
- AVOID DAMAGING FENCES, HEDGES AND WALLS.
- LEAVE NO LITTER.
- SAFEGUARD WATER SUPPLIES. Do not pollute streams, ponds or water troughs.
- PROTECT WILDLIFE, PLANTS AND TREES.
- GO CAREFULLY ON COUNTRY ROADS. Single file, facing oncoming traffic.
- RESPECT THE LIFE OF THE COUNTRYSIDE.

MAPS AND SCALES

↑

The Republic of Ireland is in the process of a complete re-survey and re-issue of its small-scale maps, changing from imperial to metric units. This has created some problems for us in that the re-survey has shown up some minor errors in heights, so that the new metric height is often not a simple conversion from the old height in feet. Where there are old maps in print as well as new ones, we have given in the text the two heights as shown on the maps, even where these are not exactly compatible; where we have only one height, be it metric or imperial, we have made a strict conversion. In a year or two this may pose a few problems for readers, in that new metric maps will have metric heights which may differ from the converted heights we have listed. This small problem is more than compensated by the better quality of the new 1:50,000 maps as compared with the old ½ inch ones.

Where heights or distances are approximate, as in 'walk 300yds along the road and turn off at a stile', we have not been pedantic and converted this to '274.3m', but, since the instruction is clearly to give an approximate distance, have simply written '270m/300yds'.

While the sketch maps in this book will give you a good idea of your route, they are hardly sufficient, especially on the more mountainous walks, as complete guides, and you are strongly advised to use the relevant topographical map. The maps available in the spring of 1991 are as follows:

Ordnance Survey maps:

1:250,000 Holiday map. Sheet 4
(These are suitable for general planning.)
Half-inch to 1 mile (1:126,720) maps. Sheets 20, 21 and 24
(These are out-of-date, and really too small for walkers, but in many areas they are the only maps available.)
1 inch to 1 mile (1:63,360) map. Sheet Killarney District
(Beware! The contour interval changes from 100ft (30m) below 1,000ft (300m) to 250ft (75m) above 1,000ft.)
1:50,000 (1¼ ins to 1 mile) map. Sheet 78
(These maps are up-to-date, and of good quality; further sheets are being issued, so you should enquire if any more are available.)

Other useful maps:
MacGillycuddy's Reeks (1:25,000)
Killarney National Park (1:25,000)
Kerry Way Map Guide (1:50,000)

Walking Times
Walking times have been calculated on the basis of 4km per hour, and 400m ascent per hour. This is roughly equivalent to 2½ miles per hour, and 1,300ft ascent per hour. These are fairly generous, and should allow you

the occasional stop to admire the view, look at the map, take photographs, or recover your breath. They do not allow for protracted lunch stops! Extra time has been allowed if the going is difficult, and vice versa.

CLIMATE AND WEATHER

The climate and weather of the Southwest of Ireland have profound influence on human activities, including hill walking, and those venturing into the hills should have some knowledge and understanding of the conditions they are likely to meet.

The climate of western Ireland is largely the product of a westerly atmospheric circulation, and its proximity to the Atlantic Ocean. These two factors interact to give us westerly winds, mild damp weather and a narrow temperature range throughout the year.

Although the weather is highly variable there are a number of climatic features which appear to occur fairly regularly. During December and January there is a well-established low pressure system over the Atlantic spawning depressions which move rapidly eastwards, bringing strong winds and abundant frontal rain. By late January the cold anti-cyclonic weather centred over Europe may be extending westwards into Ireland giving dry, cold spells, eminently suitable for hill walking. From February to June, the cold European anti-cyclones, reinforced sometimes by a southward extension of the Greenland anti-cyclone, tend to produce the driest period of the year. Towards late June or early July pressure rises over the ocean and falls over the continent, initiating a westerly, water-laden airflow over Ireland. Cloud cover, humidity and rainfall increase and thunder becomes more prevalent, particularly during the warmer periods of August. Cold northerly air may bring active depressions in late August and September, but these can be interrupted by spells of anti-cyclonic weather. In October and November, rain-laden westerlies predominate, although an incursion of anti-cyclonic conditions can bring good daytime weather.

Prevailing winds are south-westerly and westerly but winds from the north and east may occur in anti-cyclonic conditions. The winds are lightest from June to September, and strongest from November to March, with January producing some of the severest gales in recent years.

May tends to be the sunniest month with an average of 6–7 hours of bright sunshine per day. Surprisingly, however, July tends to be relatively dull, with less sunshine then either June or August.

Snow is fairly uncommon in our maritime climate, occurring in brief spells usually in January and February, although it does occur on the high tops and in sheltered north-facing corries from November to April, and occasionally into May.

Looking specifically at West Cork/Kerry, we find that it is marginally warmer than the rest of the west coast, the mean annual temperature at Cahirciveen Observatory in the period 1931-60 being 10.8°C. The rainfall is typical of the west with the lowlands receiving 1,250 to 2,000 mm (50 to 80 inches) of rain per annum and the mountains receiving 2,000 to 3,000 mm (80 to 120 inches). Actual rainy days (when more than 0.2 mm of rain falls) number 200 to 250 days each year. It is not a coincidence that the Caha

Mountains are named after *ceatha*, the Irish word for showers. Waterproofs are an essential part of any walker's gear but the position is not as bleak as this may indicate. Rain rarely falls for more than a few hours each day and the striking feature is the difference from day to day, with great change within the narrow limits of our climate. In the words of T.J. Barrington in his *Discovering Kerry*, the area has little climate but much weather. Even the dullest days can generally be used for lower-level walks while one awaits perfect conditions for high-level outings.

INTRODUCTION

First Edition

My own hill walking began in my schooldays, prompted by the fact that Carrauntuohill, Ireland's highest peak, was for us, living in Killorglin, virtually on our doorstep. Like others, we climbed mountains simply because they were there. Continued walking led to an enjoyment of the achievement and the opportunity for discovery. Later, there was the physical challenge, firstly in pushing oneself to one's limits and secondly in perfecting the ability to navigate. The thrill of setting a course through fog or storm and arriving exactly where one intended is very real but is, of course, reserved for those who have acquired the ability to use map and compass and the feeling for the terrain. It is only now that I am acquiring an appreciation of the details of flora and fauna which adds so much to one's enjoyment. Also, there is the knowledge that hill walking is a lifelong activity — the Kerry mountaineering community includes a number of active walkers over 60 and at least one over 70. There is always the discovery of new routes and the revising of old and favoured friends. But on each individual outing, the immediate pleasure is the so necessary sense of peace, isolation and blessed escape from concrete, asphalt and the trappings of modern technology. In the lonely glens, among the dramatic coombes and on the summits, this need to replenish the soul is so easily fulfilled. Strangely enough, the welcome loneliness of the West Cork/Kerry hills and mountains is emphasised by the fact that even on the highest ground, there are still signs of human contact.

This guide is basically a series of route descriptions intended to enable people to find their way on and off the hills. It should be of use to those new to hill walking or experienced walkers new to this region's hills which, fortunately or unfortunately depending on your viewpoint, are still a very much underused amenity. It provides only a sample of what West Cork and Kerry can offer and I make no claim that even all the main walks are included. However, those described provide an introduction and readers will, no doubt, later wish to depart from the guide and engage in the discovery of new ground for themselves.

The walks described range from short explanatory rambles, sometimes along green roads, suitable for family groups (for example, Walks 7(b), 35, 42) to longer outings (2, 20, 21) which should only be attempted by those with experience. No attempt has been made to distinguish between 'safe' routes, those which might be dangerous — for example if there was a change in weather — and those which are inherently dangerous due to the existence of cliffs and narrow ridges. Among the latter would be Walks 18, 19, 20, 21, 23, 46, 47 in particular. It is best to regard all walks as requiring care. Remember that a simple ankle sprain can lead to a night on the mountain and, at worst, death by exposure. In the descriptions, I have usually plotted a route up steeper ground and down the more gradual slope (see Walk 23) in the belief that the descent is for many more trying than the ascent.

The times suggested are the main measuring yardstick but even these can only be taken as very rough guides. Obviously, the determination of the party, what they are carrying and the weather will determine the actual time on each individual outing.

The region is covered by three 1:126,720 (half inch to one mile) Ordnance survey maps. These are sheets No. 20 (Dingle Bay), No. 21 (Cork-Kerry) and No. 24 (West Cork). There is also a very useful and more informative 1:63,360 (one inch to one mile) Ordnance Survey sheet, called the Killarney District, covering much of the centre of Kerry, including Mangerton and the MacGillycuddy's Reeks and also extending down to include a substantial part of the Beara Peninsula.

To facilitate use of the OS maps, a grid reference is given for each Walk starting point, or points if there are more than one. A six-figure reference has been provided but particularly with the ½" sheets, a four-figure reference may be easier for the reader. This can be achieved by simply discarding the third figures in each case. For example, in Walk No. 1 the starting point is given as 090 657. This could also be read as 09 65 and this may make is simpler to pinpoint the spot on the ½" OS sheet No. 21, which incidentally also gives as an aid examples of grid references for two prominent features.

In the course of the walks, I have used compass points (southwest; east-northeast, etc.). These, I feel, would be more reliable direction indicators than suggesting travelling right or left as the case may be. In any case, a person might turn about, perhaps to admire the view and right or left would no longer be valid.

The term Green Road appears in the text on a number of occasions. As used, it refers to any unsurfaced road, whether grassed-over or not, which does not lead to an inhabited house. Thus, I have applied to it, among others, roads to peat bogs and disused arteries of former times. Incidentally, as the OS maps warn, the indication of a path does not grant an automatic right of way and this prompts me to make a few suggestions on behaviour on the way to and from the hills and mountains.

It is generally accepted that no restraint is placed on walkers along the hill and mountain tops and unlike the situation in other countries, we are not confined to particular paths. This facility should not, however, be abused. Where there are fences, care should be taken not to cause any damage. Any stones knocked should be replaced and wire sheep fencing (very expensive these days) should be treated with the utmost respect. It is surprising how many people actually stand on the strands of wire while crossing. This is a cardinal sin and should never be practised. Always look for a gate or usable crossing point. Sheep themselves are also valuable assets in the wilder terrain of the region. On no account should a dog be taken on a walk, particularly in the lambing season. Even if the pet is considered totally uninterested in a chase, its behaviour may frighten sheep onto dangerous ground. If a dog must for some reason accompany the owner, it should always be kept on a lead. The practice of tumbling rocks can also frighten animals and should be avoided — it could also be a source of danger to humans. Need I mention that all sweet and chocolate wrappings should be put in the pocket and all cans, plastic bags, etc., taken home in the knapsack? In short, the mountain area should be left as you found it, both for the benefit of the owners and of later users. You would like to see the area unspoiled and should allow others a similar enjoyment.

It is on the lower ground that you will generally meet the inhabitants. It is not just because I am of their stock that I regard these as a noble and gentle people, still imbued with old-world courtesy and pleased to meet visitors. Please do not pass in surly silence. At least, exchange greetings and unless it means interrupting work, you might consider pausing for a chat. Please be sure to close all gates after you and if you must go though fields, travel close to the fence to avoid damage to crops. Once again, no rubbish.

In wishing you good walking, may I protect myself by saying that while I have been as careful as time permitted in compiling the Guide, I take no responsibility for the reader's failure to travel in safety. Before you set off, please study carefully the notes on Mountain Safety.

I am very grateful to the many people who so willingly gave help while I compiled this Guide. Firstly, my thanks to those who satisfied my interest in folklore: Rev. John Hayes, formerly of Glenbeigh and now in Africa; Stephen O'Shea of Kilgobnet; Paddy Cremin of Tomies; Jim Corkery, Inchigeela and Christy Lucey, Gougane Barra; Dick Smyth, Lauragh; Eamonn and Brid Langford, Kells; Mrs Tom Shortt, Cahirciveen; Mrs Tom O'Shea, Glenmore and Waterville; Jimmy Cronin and Jim Nagle, Headford; Justin McCarthy, Cahir, Tipperary.

On Flora, I have mentioned elsewhere my thanks to Bernard Goggin of Dingle and also to Frank McGourty of Cork and, once again, Justin McCarthy. Mrs Pat Smith of Tralee, as well as joining on many outings, shared her love of nature. Frank King of Tralee, a dedicated ornithologist, provided the material on birds — I can only hope that I have been faithful to his word.

I am particularly grateful to all those who have regularly joined me on the hills over a number of years and while the Guide was being compiled — especially my colleagues in the Laune Mountaineering Club and the Kerry Mountain Rescue Team. My thanks are also due to Joss Lynam for asking me to write this Guide and for his half and encouragement during its preparation.

My brother, Gearoid, checked the typed script for errors, particularly in navigation — it is so easy for the hand to say southwest while the mind is saying southeast. Hannah Stack typed much of the manuscript.

Finally, my sincere thanks to Marguerite for help, encouragement and understanding while the pressure was on.

April 1978

New Edition

The second edition of the Guide is an expansion of the original. The main change is the addition of the two existing low-level Long Distance Walking Routes (LDWRs), the Kerry Way and the Dingle Way, to provide family walking or a relief from the serious high-level climbs.

Some of the walks included earlier have been incorporated into the LSWRs and the other high-level walk descriptions have been altered where required. At this point, I should mention that it is impossible to be entirely up-to-date. The actual shape of the hills have aided the building of farm roads and the erection of sheep fencing. You should not rely completely on such features as they may have appeared since the walk description was written. However, where mentioned in the text, they are unlikely to have disappeared and can be used with discretion as a guide.

Walking is much more than taking exercise and refining skills such as navigation. It is also an exploration of the landscape and wildlife as well as of archaeology, history and folklore. At a time when the lines of demarcation between the professionals in the natural sciences are blurring — the geographer is now into demography and the archaeologist needs the help of the botanist in the study of pollen — we can indulge any or every interest. In the hope of adding to your enjoyment, I have expanded the treatment of each topic, relating them where possible to specific walks. Let me emphasise, however, that I make no claim to expertise or to being exhaustive. The intention is simply to give background and to whet the appetite. Those wishing to delve further into any field should find suitable reference works in the bibliography at the end of the book. For the amateur or professional geologist, I can offer no better advice than to take along Ralph Horne's invaluable guide to the Dingle Peninsula. Those into archaeology can refer to the *Dingle Archaeological Survey Report* but it is hardly a book for the pocket! A similar report is in preparation following completion of the Iveragh Peninsula survey and by the time of reading may be available.

I am sure that you will enjoy using the Kerry and Dingle Ways. Where possible, old butter roads, droving paths and carriage routes have been used with the result that truly you are walking through history. Aside from benefiting from the magnificent views, you may have time to indulge in interests such as biology. Some may wish to walk the entire route — approximately 215km/135miles for the Kerry Way and 165km/100miles for the Dingle Way. However, most people will only walk a section at a time and all should be aware that while each description in this guide covers a stage between centres of population, some should be broken down into comfortable distances. In general, it should be possible to take along children if they are used to walking. Check the suitability of any stretch in the text in advance, both from the point of view of length and features, for example the height of mountain passes which are used from time to time. I find it difficult to advise on clothing — wellington boots, perhaps short ones, or light walking boots may be more suitable than heavy climbing ones. Waterproof clothing is essential and given the distance from habitations at times, it would be as well to take with you the items normally associated with the hills — map, compass, whistle, spare clothing and food, etc.

Those who enjoy the LDWRs would, I am sure, wish to have tribute paid to those who created the network. Firstly, thanks must go to all the landowners, whether private owners, the National Park or Coillte Teoranta (the Irish Forestry Board), for their co-operation. Please respect this by obeying all courtesies.

Many plotted and worked on the route of the Kerry Way and in giving the names of my colleagues on the committee, I not only note their contribution but also give you possible contacts. However, you must understand that all have full-time occupations outside of a number of voluntary involvements. These include forester P.J. Bruton of Killarney who, as well as creating the original route from Killarney across the face of Torc (temporarily out of use — a pity because of the spectacular viewing points — and hopefully to be incorporated again), also gave advice and encouragement as well as expertise in designing bridges and the like all along the route. When I first mooted the idea, as well as the sponsorship of An Taisce and the Laune Mountaineering Club, there was help from all the mountaineering fraternity of Kerry, in particular Catherine McMullin of Killorglin, in developing what became the model, the first stage to Glenbeigh. Sgt Micheal Griffin and the members of Glenbeigh Community Council took over from there. The Cahirciveen area produced workers such as John Murphy, Liam O'Connell and Paddy Cronin. Since his retirement from the Meteorological Service, Paddy has become virtually a full-time worker and many visitors enjoy his company on walks. The Waterville area was lucky to have Tom Horgan and Paddy de Buis as organisers. Belinda Baldock, as well as acting as a vigilant protector of wildlife, brought together a hard-working band of followers in the Caherdaniel area. Jim Looney in Sneem found time from community commitments to work, with assistance from Mossie Walsh. In Kenmare, a group led by Michael Murphy and Bernie O'Driscoll is still doing trojan work. Indeed, work is ongoing still in a number of areas. A direct route from Waterville to Caherdaniel is planned as is one taking in Kells Bay. A link between the Kerry Way and the Dingle Way through Killorglin, Miltown and Castlemaine is being surveyed at present.

The Dingle Way Committee also had the assistance of many from time to time. The principals involved in developing the route to Dingle were Jim Costello, Tom Finn and Sean Kelly. The Way west and north of there was in the capable hands of T.P. O Concubhain and Maurice Sheehy. For your benefit, work is still in progress, including the provision of foot-bridges where necessary.

A feature of both LDWR committees was the enthusiastic participation of various statutory bodies in what were originally community groups. FAS through Jerry Horgan provided workers under Social Employment Schemes and John O'Keeffe's help is also noted. The County Manager, Tom Collins and other staff of Kerry County Council gave invaluable help including administering the SES, and provided us with two Clerks of Work who sent well beyond the call of duty — Tommy Murphy in the Cahirciveen area and Martin Griffin on the Dingle Way. Brendan O'Connor has sat on both LDWR committees as the local authority representa-tive, ironing out various problems. John Ashe fulfilled the same function on behalf of County Kerry Vocational Education Committee through whom sporting grants are channeled. Cospoir, the Sports Council, and its National Long Distance Walking Routes Committee provided these National Lottery funds as well as essential advice and Bord Failte Eireann also supported. On a local level, Declan Murphy of Cork/Kerry Tourism has acted as hard-working secretary to both committees following the tradition of his predecessor, Liam O'Hanlon and his Manager, Con O Conaill. The staff of Killarney National Park through Jim Larner are always helpful and encouraging, as are the staff of Coillte Teoranta.

I need not repeat those mentioned in the original preface but would add thanks to all who have walked with me over the years. I hope you get as much enjoyment as we have.

January 1991

Access and Accommodation

The Southwest of Ireland is served by two international airports. Shannon has flights to and from North and South America. Closer is Cork (approx-imately 100km/60miles), offering Aer Lingus service from London, Manchester, Birmingham, Paris, Renne and Jersey, and Ryanair from Luton. Much closer to the walking routes (for example, 16km/10miles from Killarney/Killorglin/Tralee) is the regional airport at Farranfore which at present offers flights to and from Dublin as well as an Aer Lingus service from London and a Ryanair from Luton.

The car ferry services are, direct from Britain, Swansea Cork Ferries (Swansea/Cork), B & I Line (Pembroke/Rosslare) and Sealink British Ferries (Fishguard/Rosslare). Direct from mainland Europe, the services are Irish Ferries (Le Havre/Cork, Le Havre/Rosslare and Cherbourg/Rosslare) and Brittany Ferries (Rosscoff/Cork).

Internal transport is provided by Irish Rail (services to Killarney and Tralee) and Bus Eireann (network to the towns and villages).

The Cork/Kerry region is the main tourist area in the country. Thus, there is a wide selection of accommodation to choose from, ranging from castles to modern hotels to family-run premises. Guesthouses offer a personal service in a more intimate atmosphere. In farmhouse and in town and country homes, you can stay with an Irish family in locations as diverse as the large city/town and the heart of the country. There are youth hostels (Irish Youth Hostel Association) and a network of privately-owned hostels. Caravan and camping parks are becoming more widespread and luxurious. There is also a wide range of self-catering properties in many different locations. In summary, where you stay depends on preference and budget. In the first edition of this Guide, I recommended establishments, particularly in areas where accommodation was scarce. Now, the network is so developed that the best suggestion is to get an up-to-date list from Cork/Kerry Tourism either at the Tourist Office, Grand Parade, Cork City (Tel. 021–273251, Fax 021–273504) or the Tourist Office, Town Hall, Killarney, Co. Kerry (Tel. 064–31633, Fax 064–34506). Any other queries regarding transport, car hire, etc., will also get prompt attention.

Geology and Geomorphology

The science of geology/geomorphology is still developing and, as I understand it, there is current debate on dating and sequence, for example of the various interglacial periods. You must accept a simplistic approach. My excuse is that experts have yet to clarify matters but the truth is, of course, that my knowledge is rather scanty!

The area of West Cork and Kerry originally consisted of beds of Old Red Sandstone covered by beds of limestone, laid down at various times, say 345-390 million years ago, under either freshwater lakes or a raised sea. Some volcanic activity also occurred — visible today at Bennaunmore south of Lough Guitane to the east of Killarney (Walk 13) and Clogher Head/Minnaunmore on the Dingle Peninsula (Walk 45) as well as on the Beara Peninsula at Black Ball Head (Walk 5). For our pursuit of walking, however, we need not concern ourselves too much with geology (the nature of rocks and other elements of the earth's crust) but we are very interested in geomorphology (the shape of that crust) as that is what makes the more demanding aspects of our pastime possible.

The actual mountain-building process occurred mainly 290 million years ago when large-scale movement in the earth's crust caused what has often been described as a corrugated-iron effect. The folding brought the harder sandstone alongside the less durable limestone. A major fault (a rupture in the earth's crust) thrust what is now the northern slope of the MacGillycuddy's Reeks even higher above the neighbouring rocks. The folds were mainly east-west across Ireland, being very obvious along the line of the Dingle Peninsula. However, a broadening of the folds towards the west resulted in a north-east to south-west orientation in the Iveragh Peninsula and in West Cork. A later tilting, some 26 million years ago, gave the region not only the highest peaks in Ireland but also the greatest concentration of mountains. For example, the Iveragh Peninsula contains 120 mountains, forty of them Munros — exceeding the magical 610m/2,000ft — with eight peaks over 915m/3,000ft.

Erosion followed the folding. The softer limestone disappeared from the higher ground, exposing the sandstone and what little volcanic material there was to create the hills and cliffs that we now have. Limestone still blankets the lower ground but it also was worn sufficiently to deepen the valleys which were later drowned to create the present bays. This brings the sea well inland and the contrast, whether it be of steep cliff dropping to rolling waves as at Slea Head (Walk 43) or the distant glimpse of water from an inland peak, is one of the attractions to hill walkers. The limestone is not a flat bed and a line of projecting rocks seen in the sea east from Fenit and terminating as the Magharee Islands helped to create the Castlegregory spit — a tombolo of sand and shingle connecting Fahamore/Kilshannig (Walk 49) with the mainland. Erosion of limestone shorelines of Killarney's Lough Leane and Muckross Lake (Walk 13) has created the fantastic shapes which have provided material for the jaunting car driver's tall tales.

But it was glaciation during the Ice Age which gave the present character to the hills and mountains. It seems that there were repeated alternating periods of freezing and warming but it is accepted generally that there was one phase, approximately 150,000 years ago, when ice sheets covered most of Ireland. These mantled the country with boulder clay, sands and gravels. A later glaciation, say 70,000 years ago, affected the northern and eastern parts of Ireland but did not spread to this region. However, the southwest was sufficiently high to create its own snow and ice fields and it seems that it was this later phase which carved the features to be seen today. Indeed, the Ice Age effect is so distinct in Ireland, particularly in the southwest, that Irish terms, for example *cum* (coombe), are used internationally to describe features.

Typically, a coombe was created from an existing rock basin which filled with snow. This, due to weight and compression, turned to ice which deepened the basin and pushed fragments from the back wall forward to create a fragile moraine, which often acts as a water dam. Examples of coombes, large and small, and moraine-trapped lakes are to be found in all the hill ranges. The Caha Mountains in Beara have a series of long, narrow coombe valleys along their northwestern side, some with spectacular waterfalls on the back wall, for example Glaninchiquin (Walk 6). In the Iveragh and Dingle Peninsulas, the coombes also are almost all on the northern (understandably the sunless and colder) side. The Hag's Glen (Walk 18a) the conventional approach to Carrauntuohill, is a particularly good example, having a number of smaller 'hanging' coombes, some rising above one another in Cummeenoughter and also offering in the Hag's Teeth an example of truncated spurs, cut by the moving glacier. The most dramatic expression is where two coombes have been carved back, to create an arête and give a challenging knife-edge walk, such as over Cummeenapeasta Lake on the MacGillycuddy's Reeks Ridge (Walk 20) or between Beenkeragh and Carrauntuohill (Walk 19). Some valleys have a series of lakes, each lower than its neighbour, joined by streams and these are termed ribbon or paternoster lakes, the latter due to the similarity to prayer beads. Examples are again Glaninchiquin (Walk 6), Coomloughra (Walk 19) on the eastern side of Carrauntuohill, the Horses' Glen (Walk 12) and, of course, the eastern approach to Mount Brandon (Walk 46) which still looks so freshly carved. Incidentally, at one stage, coombes were thought to be extinct volcanoes. Near the Conair Pass (the end of Walk 47) is Lough Doon (The Pedlar's Lake) where in 1849 evidence of ice action in Ireland was first reported. It is worth a visit, both for its perfection and historical significance.

The many high passes now carrying roads through the mountains were created by ice movement. A large regional ice sheet centred at Templenoe on the northern shore of Kenmare River/Bay (Walk 33) spread out north/northeast to create the Gap of Dunloe, Moll's Gap and the Windy Gap (Walk 34) and north/northwest to carve out Ballaghbeama (Walk 21a) as well as the Black Valley (Walk 17) and the Caragh River valley. The Gap of Dunloe (Walks 15/20) is also an example of watershed breaching — the ice movement changed the course of the water drainage from east-west to the present-day south-north river flow. As mentioned in the text, the dramatic carving effect is best appreciated when viewed from afar, from the south at Glaninchiquin (Walk 6) and from the north at Caragh Lake (Walk 22).

It is accepted that some of the high ground stood as nunataks above the ice during both phases. This has left a smooth top on many summits and ridges, such as the Caha Mountains (Walk 8), Mangerton (Walk 11) and Coomasaharn (Walk 23) or rocks grotesquely cracked and split by frost such as on the MacGillycuddy's Reeks (Walks 19/20) and the Brandon Ridge (Walk 47).

A milder climate after the Ice Age gave Ireland its forests and blanket of bog — both important elements of the landscape from the walker's point of view.

Flora and Fauna

Flora   After the Ice Age, primitive plants developed and the decay in time produced clay. Today, the southwest of Ireland has a number of rare Lusitanian plants. The theory is that the disappearing ice cover allowed the land to rise and that there was a land bridge to assist migration of the plants which are otherwise natives only of Spain and Portugal. Found on the mountains are St Patrick's cabbage (*Saxifraga spathularis*) — a relation of the garden-dwelling London Pride and found growing on rocks up to a high level, for example on the MacGillycuddy's Reeks Ridge (Walks 19/20) — and its companion, the kidney saxifrage (*Saxifraga hirsuta*). Irish spurge (*Euphorbia hyberna*) is to be seen along streams benefiting from the lime-free soil.

Except for wetlands and the mountain tops, in time Ireland became covered from coast to coast in forest. Oak and elm replaced the earlier willow, juniper, birch and hazel. The Scot's pine was also a native, now seen as bog deal in cut-away peat. Little remains of the ancient oak woods other than Derrycunnihy (Walks 13/33) and perhaps Lickeen (Walk 22). A feature of these woods is the rhododendron which, while colourful in flower and an addition to photographs and postcards, is now recognised as a pest and is being eliminated, with much difficulty it must be said. Killarney, with Gougane Barra (Walk 1), is famous for the arbutus (*Arbutus unedo*), also known as the strawberry-tree, which like other Mediterranean plants has flourished better in this area than in its homeland.

Elsewhere, the dominant trees in today's natural woodland in the southwest are sessile oak (*Quercus petraea*) and birch (*Betula pubescens*), the first forming the top (canopy) layer and the second joining holly (*Ilex aquifolium*) and hazel (*Corylus avellana*) to create the shrub layer. The mountain ash or rowan tree (*Sorbus aucuparia*) with its sprays of red berry is a particular favourite of mine, to be found with birch in isolated stands as well as in woodland. The lower (field) layer consists of bracken and woodrush with a ground layer of mosses and small ferns. The Killarney fern is so rare that its locations are kept a tight secret. Flowers bloom early in the year to avail of the light and sun before the canopy of leaves develops. The most obvious example is the bluebell (*Endymion non-scriptus*). The profusion of lichens on the trees vouches for the purity of the air. Aside from a rich insect life, woodland provides shelter for birds such as woodpigeon (*Columba palumbus*), seen particularly where there are holly trees. Another woodland resident is the goldcrest (*Regulus regulus*) as are the common robin (*Erithacus rubecula*), chaffinch (*Fringilla coelebes*) and bluetit (*Parus caeruleus*).

As man successively cleared areas of trees, bog developed and in time, came to blanket much of the land. Putting it at its simplest, peat growth commences in shallow stagnant lake edges. Remains of pondweeds, waterlilies, etc., accumulate and, gradually, growth rises above the level of the groundwater. The acidity of developing bog mosses assists drying out and the cycle is complete. Most of the terrain used by walkers consists either of bogland (where vegetation is rooted in the peat) or heathland (generally sloping drained land where the vegetation is rooted in soil) and these environments are worth some attention.

Much of the vegetation is common to both bogland and heathland. There are two types of gorse/furze, generally growing on earthen fences — the common furze (*Ulex europaeus*) and the autumn or dwarf furze (*Ulex galli*) — and their differing flowering seasons means that a riot of yellow is present most of the year. The contrasting purple of late summer and autumn is provided by the other obvious occupant of both habitats — bell heather (*Erica cinerea*) and ling heather (*Calluna vulgaris*). Various grasses on the lower ground provide feeding for sheep, if not invaded by bracken

(*Pteridium aquilinium*). The dominant plant in bogland are the *Sphagnum* mosses forming a sponge of various colours. This moss was used to treat wounds received in battle, even up to World War I. The sponge absorbed blood and the acidity sterilised. Bog cotton (*Eriophorum angustifolium*) is easily identified by the white whisker and bog rush (*Schoenus nigricans*) is a distinctive plant of western blanket bogs. Of the flowers, the purple of wild orchid (*Dactylorhiza majalis*) is a regular sighting. On drier ground, fruit in the form of the ground-hugging whortleberry or hurt can be found. This is said to be a cousin of the American blueberry but not as large.

The lack of nitrogen in the soil is the reason for two other interesting plants which are carniverous, i.e. meat eating. It is a cause of much surprise to most people to learn of the existence of such plants in Ireland as the imagination immediately conjures up visions of vast man-eating monsters so beloved of film makers. However, these are small and attractive plants which do nothing more than trap and absorb insects, easily seen on inspection of the leaves. They are the great butterwort (*Pinguicula grandiflora*) — also a Lusitanian plant — and the sundew (*Drosera*), both of which are to be found frequently in large numbers in wet ground. The great butterworth looks like a light green starfish hugging the ground and it sports a violet flower on a tall stem (May-July). The hairs on the sundew's spatula-shaped leaves give it a red/orange appearance.

Bogland — once regarded as empty wasteland — has acquired the status of an endangered species, having disappeared from much of Europe. Dr David Bellamy in his book outlines the attractions of this habitat in his own enthusiastic way and among his recommendation for conservation are the Lowland Blanket Bog between Ballaghisheen and Bealalaw Bridge in Glencar (Walk 22) and the Mountain Blanket Bog on Mangerton (Walk 11).

The specialist in the rarer mountain plants should visit the east face of Mount Brandon (Walk 46), which boasts a concentration and richness of Arctic/Alpine flora, some of them at their most southerly extension in Ireland. I can give no better advice than that he or she contact Bernard Goggin of Dingle who has made a study. Bernard might object to being termed an expert but his knowledge is a cause of wonder to one so ignorant as myself. He is willing always to talk to somebody sharing his interest.

Fauna   Animals to be seen — aside from grazing sheep and cattle — include rabbits, very plentiful in some places, for example at Loch Chill Uru (Walk 44b). Hares are also plentiful and they have been seen in winter turned partly white on Mount Brandon (Walks 46/47) with reports of all-white ones in the Beenoskee area (Walk 40). Stoats are to be found everywhere as are foxes — although these may be smelt in the passing wind, if you know how, rather than be seen. There are many hedgehogs and shrews, and wood and field mice aplenty. Bank voles are recent immigrants. Goats are to be seen in many areas, some wild and some semi-tame. There is a herd of black and white goats in the Mangerton area (Walk 11) and another herd on Coumduff (Walk 26).

Killarney is, of course, famous for its deer. The Irish Red Deer is now unique to the area and can be seen around Mangerton-Torc (Walks 11b/ 13/14), which incidentally is also the haunt of the red squirrel. The smaller Japanese sika deer can be seen over a wider area, including the western side of the Killarney Lakes. Both species are to be seen on higher ground in the summer. The distinctive black Kerry Cow may be seen grazing in this area also.

Frog-spawn can be found in bog pools. Mountains lakes, generally low in nutrients, may be devoid of fish life. Plants consist mainly of duckweeds (*Lemna*) and the most conspicuous is the water lily (*Nymphaea alba*). Slugs are always plentiful in the damp climate. Unique to the area (outside of Spain and Portugal) is the greater spotted slug of Kerry, shiney black with silver spots, to be seen feeding on lichen on rocks after rain. Perhaps this animal is honoured in the placename met on the MacGillycuddy's Reeks Ridge (Walk 20), Coomeenapeasta (*Coimin na Peiste*) which could be translated as the Coombe of the slug or of the Serpent. The reference, thus, could be to the legendary Carrabuncle, a Loch Ness-type serpent, said to inhabit Lough Gael under the Brandon Ridge (Walk 47). Similar stories exist regarding Lough Brin, seen from Mullaghanattin (Walk 21) and Lough Iskanagahiny (Walk 27). I know of no one who has actually seen the beast, so you can afford to keep an eye out for the more obvious bird life!

The hills of the southwest are rich in bird life and some birds are of particular interest to ornithologists. One such is the chough (*Pyrrhocorax pyrrhocorax*), generally a Mediterranean resident but now plentiful in the area and recognised from its 'chuff' call.

Other residents are the jay (*Garrulus glandarius*), a recent breeder here, the red grouse (*Lagopus lagopus*) and the dipper (*Cinclus cinclus*), the last to be seen near streams or perhaps walking underwater if the pool is clear. There are separate Irish races of these three birds. The grey wagtail (*Motacilla cinerea*) may be seen in company with the dipper.

Birds of prey are represented by the peregrine falcon (*Falco peregrinus*) (there are examples of this endangered species but those in the know obviously are not saying where), the kestrel (*Falco tinnunculus*) and the merlin (*Falco columbarius*). The carrion grey crow (*Corvus corone cornix*) is very successful due to its adaptability in nesting either in heather or in trees and despite its unpopularity with game preservers, is a useful scavenger, for example in picking clean sheep corpses. The twite (*Acanthis flavirostris*) — not otherwise widespread in Europe — nests in heather. The raven (*Corvus corax*) is to be found on almost all cliffs and for many years, there has been a remarkably large colony (over 100) on the cliff over Lough Doon (Pedlar's Lake) near the Conair Pass (end of Walk 47). The rock dove (*Columba livia*) usually resides on sea coasts and islands but the only mountain nesting ones observed in Ireland are in Derrymore Glen (Walk 35).

In summer, the meadow pipit (*Anthus pratensis*) and the skylark (*Alauda arvensis*) move to the hills from lower ground. Summer visitors from abroad are the wheatear (*Oenanthe oenanthe*), the swift (*Apus apus*) and the house martin (*Delichon urbica*). The last might not be regarded as a hill bird but for a number of years there has been a colony near the rock-climbing faces near Loo Bridge, east of Bennaunmore (Walk 10). These are the only house martins in Kerry using a natural site. They nest on the dry section of these inland cliffs, returning to the habitat of their ancestors instead of using the usual nesting places, house eaves and bridges.

The corncrake (*Crex crex*) was a common summer visitor but changing farming practices here, as elsewhere in Europe, have meant virtual disappearance. I have been told of its survival in farmland close to Bealalaw Bridge on the Kerry Way (Walk 22) but you would have to arrange a night-time trip to be sure of hearing its grating call.

In winter, the bird population is increased by visitors of some of the resident species and also by the arrival of snow bunting (*Plectrophenax nivalis*) and the whooper swan (*Cygnus cygnus*). The white-fronted goose (*Anser albifrons*) travels from Greenland to feed on the higher ground over the Killarney Upper Lake and a possible winter detour on Walk 13 is intended to avoid disturbance of its roost. The golden plover (*Charadrius apricarius*) used to nest in Kerry but is seen now only in the course of migration. The dotterel (*Charadrius morinellus*), while regarded with the peregrine falcon and the twite as a symbol of a mountain, is also a passage visitor only.

The two Long Distance Walking Routes (LDWRs) tend to follow the coast, much of the Dingle Way in particular is close to sanddune and we should look briefly at that very different habitat. Typically, the sequence is gravel beach, sand-binding marram grass on fragile parallel dune ridges and intervening slacks with, further inland, the more consolidated dunes established by grassland vegetation. The shallow water of the slacks harbours a variety of breeding birds.

A unique example is provided in the dunes just north of Stradbally (Walk 49). These are one of the few breeding and foraging grounds of the rare Lusitanian amphibian, the natterjack toad (*Bufo calamita*). This feature, coupled with the geological significance of the tombolo, the diversity of plants and the fact that they are bounded on the east by the wildlife sanctuary of a former lagoon, now the freshwater lake Lough Gill, prompted An Taisce (The National Trust for Ireland) to propose the dunes as a field study area. Unfortunately, a golf course is being developed there rather than sensibly being sited elsewhere and one must hope that damage will be limited.

All along the coast, there is a variety of shore birds and cliff dwellers, a common winter visitor being the brent goose (*Branta bernicla*). On the Kerry Way, Rossbeigh spit (Walk 24), and on the Dingle Way, Tralee Bay (Walk 38) and Inch spit (Walk 39) are sanctuaries.

The low-level LDWRs use as green roads the old lines of communication whenever possible. As well as travelling by Parknasilla (Walk 33) where exotic plants flourish in the mild climate aided by the Gulf Stream, the old roads generally have a rich hedgerow. Visitors from abroad, who have difficulty in growing fuchsia in their garden, never fail to wonder at the height and the profusion of red-bell flower achieved in the wild in this area. In autumn, the blackberry-laden bramble provides take-away sustenance. In season, the bright orange flower of the montbretia, as well as adding another layer of colour, marks the site of habitation — it was regularly used to decorate an earthen fence across the road from a cottage.

In short, there is a variety of tree, plant and animal to satisfy the expert and to interest the amateur.

History, Archaeology and Folklore

The treatment of this topic must be even more cursory. It would take volumes to cover the complexity of events and relationships influenced by human ambition and frailty. The objective here is to set objects and events mentioned in the walk descriptions in some context. A strict chronology is not observed.

We noted earlier that ancient Ireland was covered in forest from coast to coast. One exception was the mountain tops which consequently became the thoroughfares of the times and man has left his mark on what is now wilderness. There are a number of burial chambers on the hilltops, for example the Paps (Walk 9) — also a place of worship —and, possibly also, Lachtshee at Glenbeigh (Walk 24) and Dromavally, Anascaul (Walk 40). Caherconree (Walk 37) has a promontory fort, one of the few inland ones, and there are coastal ones at Eask, Dingle (Walk 42) and Fahan near Slea Head (Walk 43). There are standing stones, generally decorated, in many places, some being the remains of megalithic tombs — see *Geatai na Gloire* near Dingle (Walk 43). Writing in the form of ogham, the ancient Irish alphabet, is seen on rocks at Glenfais, Camp (Walk 38) as well as Kilcolman, Ventry (Walk 43). Rock art can be seen at Glenbeigh Coomasaharn (Walk 23) and Coolnaharrigle (Walk 24), as well as near Staigue Fort (Walk 30).

The Fianna were Ireland's legendary standing army at the time of the Roman Empire. Rome never invaded Ireland and the folly of even considering it must have been emphasised by tales of the Fianna confronting the combined armies of the King of the World and the King of Spain at the Battle of Ventry (Walk 43). The warriors of old kept in practice by fighting among themselves, the womenfolk playing their part — see Caherconree (Walk 37) and Anascaul (Walk 40). Otherwise, the Fianna passed the time in hunting, as at Derrynafeana, Glencar (Walk 17). Deer was cooked in pits in the ground, *fulachta fiadh*, such as those on the banks of the Garfinny River, Dingle (Walk 41). Fianna lore was related to Early Christian monks by the last of the Fianna, Oisin, when he returned from

Tir na nOg, the Land of Youth, and began a search for his dead companions at Ballaghinsheen, Glencar (Walk 22).

The monks and churchmen were adept at converting to their own use pagan practices and sites — even the summit of Mount Brandon (Walk 46). Their churches of various vintages can be seen along the Kerry Way at Muckross, Killarney (Walk 13), Srugreana near Cahirciveen (Walk 26) and Kilcrohane, Caherdaniel (Walk 30) and on the Dingle Way, at Killelton between Tralee and Camp (Walk 38) and *Teampall Martain* at Lispole (Walk 41) as well as Stradbally and Kilshannig churches (Walk 49). Gallarus (off Walk 45) is the finest example of a dry stone oratory. Through the Dark Ages, Irish monks took Christianity back to Europe and their wanderings included even America, St Brendan setting off from Brandon Creek (Walk 48). The treasures of the monasteries were attractive to the invading Norsemen and there are many folktales of Danes burying stolen plunder, as in the Black Valley (Walk 17). Ringforts were often termed Danes forts but it is realised now that they were no more than fortified dwellings. Stone forts — Ireland's best example at Staigue (Walk 30) and its smaller copy at Cahersavane near Waterville (Walk 28) — were a more developed form, signifying the wealth of their builders.

The Clan system prevailed, the Irish being among the first to adopt family or surnames. Clans intermarried and developed lines of communication such as *Bothairin a' Carta* (Walk 5) or were at war with one another. There was no powerful central authority, thus facilitating the Norman invasion beginning 1167, despite at least one defeat in 1262 at the hands of the McCarthys at Tooreencormick, Killarney (Walk 11a). In time, the Normans also intermarried and 'became more Irish than the Irish themselves'. Principal were the Fitzgeralds, one of whose castles stands near Murreagh (Walk 45). The English, in the course of their conquest of Ireland, fought many of their civil wars on Irish soil, the Irish looking to mainland Europe for assistance. The Spaniards came to their aid to suffer defeat at *Dun an Oir* (Walk 45) in 1580. The combined forces of Irish and Spaniards suffered defeat at the Battle of Kinsale in 1601 leading to O'Sullivan Beara's epic mid-winter march from Cork to Leitrim in 1602 (Walks 4, 5). While there were setbacks, as in the Waterville area (Walks 26, 28), Cromwell's war in Ireland was marked with more successes, leading to the destruction of many Irish castles including in 1650 Minard Castle (Walk 41). Organised plantation of Ireland with English settlers then began. Petty made the necessary survey and acquired for himself a number of desirable properties including land at Blackstones, Glencar where he set up his ironworks (Walk 22).

The Irish remained staunchly Catholic and religious suppression meant that Mass had to be celebrated in secret, often at Mass Rocks as in the Black Valley (Walk 17) and Coomasaharn, Glenbeigh (Walk 23). Education was received from travelling scholars, often in hedge schools such as those in Glenmore, Waterville (Walk 28). The first half of nineteenth-century Irish history belongs to a Kerryman, Daniel O'Connell (The Liberator). A lawyer and politician, he secured Catholic Emancipation. Also an international champion of civil rights, he was born near Cahirciveen at Carhan (Walk 24), lived at Derrynane near Caherdaniel (Walk 28) and many of the coach roads incorporated into the Kerry Way were used by him.

The traumatic event of the last century and still vivid in the folk memory was the Famine — actually a series of famines which halved Ireland's population. While the policy of *laissez faire* meant that grain was exported, the peasantry starved once the potato rotted and official charity extended only to the construction of workhouses like the one in Cahirciveen (Walks 24, 26). Fever allied with weakness meant that those who died had to be buried in unmarked graves, only occasionally in official graveyards, Killinane near Cahirciveen (Walk 26) being one. The Glenbeigh Evictions (Walk 24) and the Clearances with the destruction of bridges of the Old Kenmare Road (Walks 13, 14, 34) resulted in the widespread emigration which has given so many countries of the world a strong Irish population. Those interested in their roots might consult the archives at Blennerville Windmill complex (Walk 38), having seen nearby the reconstructed section of Tralee & Dingle Light Railway, another relic of the last century.

Ireland's War of Independence began early this century. One of the incidents, the escape of Tom Barry's Flying Column, is noted in Walk 1. Memorials to that war and the Civil War which followed can be seen at various points along the walks.

Maintaining a 'neutrality favouring the Allies' during World War II, Ireland escaped much of the effects. However, there were a number of aircraft crashes, now being recorded by the Warplane Research Group of Ireland, two on the Kerry mountains, on the MacGillycuddy's Reeks Ridge (Walk 20) and near Mount Brandon (Walk 46).

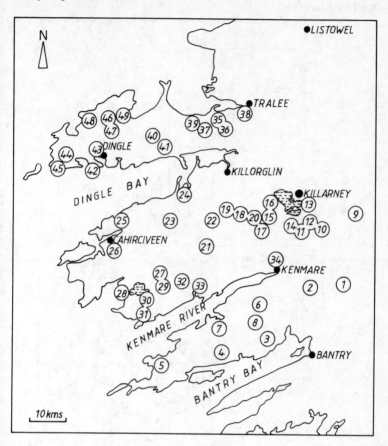

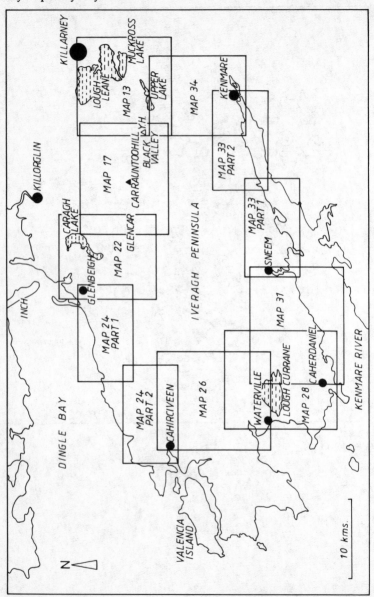

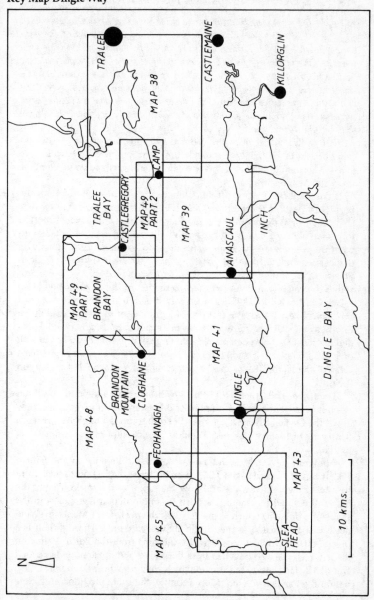

1. GOUGANE BARRA HORSESHOE

↑

Our first walk is at the source of the River Lee — the Coomroe Glen (Cum Rua, Red Coombe), generally called Gougane Barra. For anyone beginning hillwalking, this is an ideal area, thanks to the work of Coillte Teo., the Irish Forestry Board. As well as opening the forest as a National Park, the Service created a number of very attractive walks and published a booklet and a leaflet dealing with geology, wildlife, history and placenames as well as the trees and plants, both native and imported. These publications have been out of print for some time but in the expectation that they will be reprinted, I will not duplicate the information.

Our walk is a circuit of the coombe and thus higher than the walks described in the booklet mentioned above and outlined on map boards spread throughout the Park. Anyone who feels so inclined could combine this with the forest walks.

Take the R584/T64 west from Ballingeary and turn right for Gougane Barra. Just past the hotel (on left) and chapel (on right), take the gate (090 657) to the right of the toilet block (in fact a circle, with thatched roof) to follow an old road which zig-zags uphill. Pass a concrete water tank and go through a gate. At this stage, leave the road, turn your back directly on the chapel and face uphill for the first peak, Foilastookeen (*Faill a' Stuaicín*, Cliff of the Little Pinnacle). As you go in its direction, look north across the coombe and you will see, to the left of the obvious *Faill Dubh* (Black Cliff), what looks like a cross etched on a rock. From ground level this looks like a T and is in fact one of a number of hiding places known locally as a 'bealick'. The word is, in my experience, peculiar to the area and obviously an Irish one passed into English (I presume *beal lice*, mouth of a rock). This one is shown on the map as *Beillic an Lochtaigh* (perhaps Cave of the Hero). It was used at different times of trouble by men 'on the run'.

The top of Foilastookeen (518m/1,698ft) is rather indefinite until you reach it because there are a number of false summits. It gives a fine view down the Owbeg River valley, over the tiny trapped Lough Atooreen, to Bantry town, Bantry Bay and Whiddy Island with its misfortunate oil terminal.

Continuing west, descend now to a saddle and up to the 557m/1,828ft top of *Maolach* (Bald Hill), reputed to be the last nesting place in Ireland of the golden eagle and now the haunt of the raven. Again, the top is ill defined but there is a cairn (no more than a few stones in the shape of a dolmen) which seems to mark the peak. Over Maolach, swing northwest to descend to the saddle above *Poll* (Hole). Through Poll is a precipitous path which was used by pilgrims from the Borlin Valley on the left. Funerals also travelled from this valley and apparently descended east of Maolach beside the stream which emerges where the public toilets within the Park now stand. More recently, the route provided an escape from encirclement during the War of Independence for General Tom Barry and his men, who were led at night by locals with knowledge of the area and who used their rifles to form a chain on the very steep section.

Across the Borlin Valley is the splendid coombe of Lough Nambrackderg and behind it looms Caoinkeen. With views north-northwest of the MacGillycuddy's Reeks, continue north and later northeast towards the top of Bealick (538m/1,764ft). The route is across 'benches', terraces interspersed with short rock faces, a feature I always associate with the Beara Peninsula. If you keep left approaching Bealick, you gain views of the Roughty River valley, the route used by Kerry people on Gougane Sunday, the last Sunday in September, when pilgrims gathered to honour St Finbarr. Apparently, the practice was abandoned when the festive side of the event began to dominate the religious side.

A small cairn marks the top of Bealick and distinguishes it from the other false summits. From here, follow the line of the ridge east-northeast past a small lake. **On no account should a descent through the cliffs on the right be attempted.** The most easterly point of the cliff (appropriately called *Sron*, nose) will be reached and it is then possible to swing right to join the Kerry path down beside a stream to the three houses on the eastern side of Gougane Barra lake. At the gable of one of the houses, the pilgrims stacked their strong boots, exchanging them for the more dressy Sunday boots which had been tied around their necks before travelling on into the coombe. These houses also mark the end of your walk.

Distance: 10km/6miles. Ascent: 550m/1,800ft. Walking time: 4 hours.

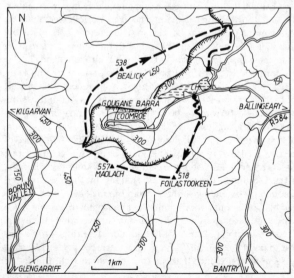

Reference OS Map: Sheet 24 (1:126,720).

2. GOUGANE BARRA-BUNANE

This walk would be suited to someone journeying between the youth hostels at Ballingeary and Bunane. The walk was devised originally by members of the Cork Mountaineering Club who proposed three days' walking over Easter weekends, connecting the Glanmore and Allihies Hostels. So far as I am aware, day 3 was never completed, because of harsh weather. This first leg is a long walk requiring some fitness but it is a very good introduction to the area, both West Cork and Kerry, the mountain ridge being the county boundary.

The start is, conveniently, that of the path called *Sli Sleibhe* (Mountain Path), one of the six Walks in the National Park, beginning from the most westerly picnic area. To reach the start, you must enter the Park, paying the standard entry charge — although you could avoid this by reversing the end of the previous Walk! Leave the picnic area by crossing a foot-bridge over one of the streams which merge in the Park to form the River Lee. Once on Sli Sleibhe, you cross the same (descending) stream three times (only two footbridges as I write but as the bottom of the path is being re-gravelled, I assume that work will continue to the top) and follow to the upper edge of the forest to emerge onto open mountain. Ascend northwest and as you reach the top of the ridge, *Muing Mor* (Wide Long-grassed Expanse) valley opens to the west ahead of you with Knockan-toreen (*Cnoc an Tuairin*, Hill of Sheep Grazing) standing to the right. The rusty red of a shed roof is clearly visible at the end. Aiming left of this, take the ridge which leads to the V of the Borlin Valley road.

From here, ascend between the coombe of Lough Nambrackderg (*Loc na mBreac Dearg*, Lake of the Red Trout — a name regularly met in mountain areas) and Caoinkeen. At first, a wire fence can be followed but you should depart from it as it swings left towards the coombe and follow the rising ground along the cliff edge until you can sit, swollen perhaps with satisfaction, at the 695m/2,280ft top, with Lough Akinkeen 425m/1,400ft below. Now turn south down to a boggy saddle and up to Knockboy (707m/2,321ft). As you ascend, a vast panorama opens both on the left and the right while behind you the MacGillycuddy's Reeks dominate the skyline to the northwest. From the peak, the whole of Bantry Bay appears to be beneath you with, on the right, Glengarriff Harbour.

Descend southwest to the Priests Leap (579m/1,898ft). A number of legends exist to explain the name. The most commonly accepted one relates how a Father James Archer SJ, in search of volunteers for the defence of the O'Sullivan Beara castle at Dunboy in 1602, was chased across the mountains by enemy soldiers. From the rock here, he is said to have jumped his horse onto a rock a mile from Bantry town. As you reach the road below, you meet an iron cross erected to commemorate the feat.

Ascend now over point 522m/1,713ft and along the ridge with a rise of 80m/250ft to point 459m/1,507ft. From here, Barraboy is clearly visible and it may seem at first glance that the course is to go right to join the shoulder up to the top. Trust the map — it is correct. Keep south of west and descend to the two lakes nestling among the rocks in the saddle below. Influenced perhaps by tales of mountain chases, one easily imagines this secluded spot to be the home of a bold rapparee. From the lakes, the line up Barraboy is obvious and from there, one can with care follow a fairly steep grassy slope down to the road and across the Bunane Bridge to the hostel.

Distance: 21km/13miles. Ascent: 1,020m/3,350ft. Walking time: 8 hours.

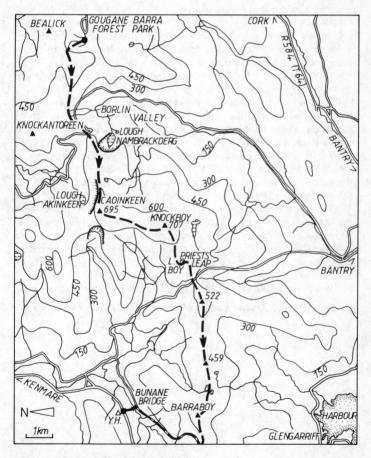

Reference OS Map: Sheet 24 (1:126,720).

3. SUGARLOAF MOUNTAIN

Approaching Glengarriff from the east along Bantry Bay, the perfect cone of the Sugarloaf Mountain, seen a few miles southwest, is inviting. It provides easy climbing and splendid views.

Some 8km/5miles from Glengarriff on the R572/L61 (Adrigole road) and less than 1km/0.5miles after the former Derrincollin School, take the road right. After 1.5km/1mile at Kealagowlane, park your car where two houses sit above the the highest point of the road snuggled into the hillside on the right (873 516).

From here, crossing the line of an old road at the 230m/750ft level, head for the shoulder left. This course avoids the short rock faces interspersed with grassy shelves which face you on the direct ascent. These are common in Beara and are locally called 'benches'. Where they are particularly precipitous, the landowners often have a herd of nimble-footed goats to clip them bare and thus deprive their sheep of the temptation of green grass. Indeed, goats can be seen on this mountain.

The shoulder provides a gentle ascent to the summit which affords one of the most spectacular panoramas possible — the rugged coastline of West Cork to the southeast and south, the might of Hungry Hill to the southwest, Iveragh Peninsula to the northwest, the Paps to the north, and, to the east, Bantry Bay laid out below you. From here, even the unfortunate Whiddy Island oil terminal, recently recommissioned for strategic storage purposes after the disastrous fire some years ago, does not offend: any tankers shrink to the size of toy boats.

From the top, other approaches are obvious. A new road pushed into the Magannagan Stream valley to the north could provide an access. A horseshoe circuit of the valley is also possible, particularly if you are based in Glengarriff and without car; it is preferable to make this circuit clockwise in order to avoid the steeper Sugarloaf, in your sight all day, as a discouraging finale.

We will retrace our steps on this occasion to the car, left at Kealagowlane.

Distance: 3.6km/2.25miles. Ascent: 440m/1,450ft. Walking time: 2 hours.

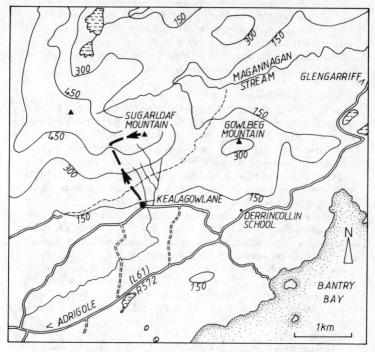

Reference OS Map: Killarney District (1:63,360).

4. HUNGRY HILL

*The sheer bulk of Hungry Hill (686m/2,251ft) dominates its sur-
roundings and, being the highest peak in the Beara Peninsula, acts as
a magnet for hillwalkers. There are a number of routes offering a climb to suit
everyone's taste. I give three routes for those new to the area while those more
experienced will be able to plot their own variations.*

4(a) From Rossmacowen

About 7km/4.5miles west of Adrigole on the R572/L61, I would disregard
the first fingerpost for Hungry Hill at the Rossmacowen River bridge and
continue past the former Rossmacowen school (now bearing a Youth
Organisation sign) and church. Turn north on the road commencing at the
gable end of the shop premises which stand beside the church, continue
north at the T-junction on surfaced road through the farmyard of Padraig
Sullivan and (seeking permission) leave your car between the house and
the sheepwire gate where it will not cause an obstruction.

From here (740 484), a green road which provides very easy walking
winds almost 3km/2miles uphill. I assume this to be a road made to give
access to the bogs for turf-cutting during World War II when fuel was
scarce. The ascent is so gentle that there is plenty of opportunity for
admiring the views all around you — Knocknagree and Maulin ahead,
Hungry Hill on your right and the expanse of Bantry Bay behind. The
Rossmacowen River valley is below you on the right and in the early stages
of the road ascent, in the inner end of the valley, you can see a house
apparently perched on an isolated rock shelf — somebody's idea of getting
away from it all.

The road takes one quickly to the 400m/1,300ft level, very close to the
Glas Loughs (*glas*, green), a generic name for small lakes high in the hills.
Even if you decide not to proceed further, the walk so far will have been
worth while. You now have views north into the Glanmore Valley and
over Kenmare River onto the Iveragh Peninsula. Bear Island (a base for
the British Fleet until 1921) still shows signs of military use — with a pair
of binoculars you will be able to see the flag pole in the army camp. The
name reminds us of the epic mid-winter march of O'Sullivan Beara who,
after the fall of Dunboy Castle, left Glengarriff on 31 December 1602 with
a band of a thousand soldiers, men, women and children, and arrived in
Leitrim with only thirty-five followers fifteen days later. The majority of
the others had died, victims of the weather, the terrain and enemies, along
the 500km/300mile route.

If that thought is not too wearying, you can continue your much
shorter journey by taking the obvious ridge east, leading up to the north
summit of Hungry Hill (656m/2,153ft). The route is roughly that of the
Cork-Kerry border — shown by the dotted line on the map: do not expect
to find a path! You meet here the greatest expression of the Beara

phenomenon — benches or rock shelves which unfortunately cross your course and seem to add to the length of the walk. However, the green road has so eased the early part of the walk and the views at this stage are so attractive that the ascent is still enjoyable. From the north summit, there is only a short rise to the main summit (686m/2,251ft) which has an Ordnance Survey trigonometrical station. The view from here, particularly over the West Cork coast with its many islands and inlets, is limited only by the visibility. The finest summer days are understandably hazy but you may have been lucky enough to travel on a day when the air is clear.

The descent on this occasion is by the way you came. It will have been obvious from the views on the ascent that you should not try to go directly from the south summit to the ridge but must return to the north summit first.

Distance: 12km/7.5miles. Ascent: 610m/2,000ft. Walking time: 4½ hours.

4(b) Coomgira Horseshoe

While the first route is the easiest one onto Hungry Hill, many walkers dislike retracing their steps and the Coomgira Horseshoe is perhaps the most usual approach.

To the south of Adrigole village on the R572/L61, two byroads lead right each side of the bridge. Take the second. Almost at the road end in Coomgira stands the stone house of John Sullivan, who has spent a lifetime sheepfarming, who knows these mountains well and whose advice on route and weather should be heeded. John was once told by a schoolmaster that the correct name of the summit ahead was Angry Hill and we assumed that the title derived from its appearance in bad weather. However, the theory now advanced is that seven of Beara's hills have been named after the seven deadly sins and that Hungry derives its name from one of these, the Irish form being *Cnoc Daod*, Hill of Envy. You can't have helped noticing that there is a magnificent waterfall on the northwest corner of this coombe and this should be kept in mind later in the day so as to resist the temptation to take a short descent.

From the house (784 493), go south to the top of the shoulder and swing northwest to ascend above what is known locally as the South Lake (Coomarkane Lake on the map) to the south summit (686m/2,251ft) of Hungry Hill. From there, cross to the north summit (656m/2,153ft) and then descend carefully to Derryclancy (556m/1,825ft). Take care that the benches do not draw you into the coombe on the right where the North Lake (Coomadavallig Lake on the map) is located. From Derryclancy, you can travel northeast to the flat plateau with old turf cuttings and then descend (southeast) the shoulder to Derreen which is across the valley from your starting place at Coomgira.

Distance: 9km/5.5miles. Ascent: 680m/2,250ft. Walking time: 4 hours.

4(c) Northern Horseshoe

For those using the Glanmore Youth Hostel, an approach from that side would obviously be more convenient.

You can walk or drive southwest almost 4km/2.5miles to the final T-junction (758 524) in the Glanmore Valley (*Gleann Mor*, Large Glen) from where you can walk into the pocket south of the 268m/878ft spur (on the map Esknamaggy). This is The Pocket; the name has been incorrectly shown on the map at Cummeengeera, in the Drimminboy River valley, to the northwest. The walk into The Pocket is beside the upper Glanmore River and I recommend leaving the road to follow the river bank and admire the many patterns eroded on the rocks. Then, ascend west beside the series of waterfalls behind the house to the flat plain of Clogher with its many meandering rivers. This is an area ideally suited to those seeking solitude — indeed, we have found the traces of what looked like a hippy encampment. Then swing south to the saddle between Knocknagree (588m/1,929ft) and point 463m/1,519ft, southeast to Glas Loughs and east up the ridge already described in 4(a) to the twin summits of Hungry Hill.

Using extreme care, a descent is just possible into The Pocket from the saddle before Derryclancy. However, I recommend going over Derryclancy (see advice in Walk 4(b) and don't be drawn into the cliffs right) and Coombane (513m/1,683ft) and across *Eisc na gCorp* to the top of the Healy Pass. Incidentally, somewhere on the ridge between Hungry Hill and the Healy Pass is a lake, possibly seasonal and not shown on the map. I have met it while travelling in thick fog (a course not recommended if unused to map and compass), am uncertain now where it is and have been told by others that they could not find it in summer. I mention it in case you get alarmed on finding it and might doubt that you were on the correct course. You can refer to Walk 7 for the story of the intriguing *Eisc na gCorp* and a description of your route down to Glanmore.

Distance (hostel to hostel): 14.5km/9miles. Ascent: 730m/2,400ft. Walking time: 5½ hours.

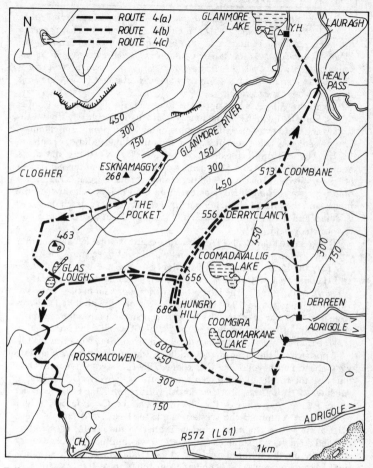

Reference OS Maps: Sheet 24 (1:126,720) or Killarney District (1:63,360).

5. ALLIHIES COPPER MINES

Features of the landscape around the picturesque village of Allihies are the chimneys and the beach at Ballydonegan, both reminders of another era. Industrial and romantic history can be sampled on a circuit of Knockgour Mountain, which gives gentle walking. However, I would caution against taking young children unless you are sure they are fit for the distance and the ascent of three passes. Surfaced road is met on a number of occasions but as there is no shop, don't forget to pack lunch.

From the village, travel northeast following the signs to the Copper Mines. Enter (591 456) left of the four Nissen huts with concrete front walls (collapsing as I write) or set your sights on the most prominent chimney. You are entering what remains of the famous Allihies Mines, opened in 1812 and by 1836 producing ore valued at £74,000 — a vast sum in today's money. Employment was 1,000 with wages ranging from the equivalent of 2p per day for girls up to £300 per annum for the Captain. Daphne du Maurier's novel *Hungry Hill* was based on the Puxleys, who owned the mines, and their neighbours. It is said by locals to be very much in accord with fact and if you have read it in advance, it will set the scene and add to your enjoyment.

The green road switchbacks uphill (disregard the first left shortly after entering). There are a number of signs warning of open mine shafts. As you rise, the view behind is of Ballydonegan Bay, the beach said to be artificial and created from the mine slag. The local name for the beach is *Tra na gCapall*, Strand of the Horses. A late development of the mines was a narrow-gauge railway. The train to carry the ore downhill had one carriage only, the rear of which was a compartment with ramp for the horse. With the aid of gravity for most of the journey downhill, the horse had to pull the train only a short distance down but, of course, all the way uphill.

Approaching the crest of the saddle, Inishfarnard Island comes into view ahead and beyond, the Caherdaniel/Sneem coast of Iveragh. Over the crest, the hamlet of Caherkeen comes into view below. Descending to Aughabrack (*Atha Breac*, Speckled Fords), you are travelling below an older route. Above, you may see the line of *Bothairin a' Carta*, (Mac)Carthy's road, which contoured the western flanks of Knockgour and Miskish. MacCarthy was a chieftain living in Eyeries to the north, his daughter married a chieftain in Allihies and the road was built to allow visits back and forth. Join the surfaced road and at the Y-junction, continue straight/right. Approximately 1km/0.6miles from the Y, take the first surfaced road right which clearly leads southeast to the saddle. Watch for and follow a green (bog) road dipping down (right) before a small bridge. Don't forget to close the gate beside a sheep-dipping tank and continue the winding course uphill.

Approaching the top, the green road goes left. Leave it on a straight course for the first (timber) forestry gate. At the Y-junction, bear left to the saddle. The view east is of Bear Haven on the near side of which is the ruin of Dunboy Castle, ancestral home of the O'Sullivan Beara, and beside it the ruin of the Puxley Castle built with the proceeds of the copper mines.

You have a choice at the saddle. Apparently a track once ran south-west from here to the summit of Knockgour over Knockoura, another of the Beara hills named after the seven deadly sins (*Cnoc Uabhair*, Hill of Pride). However, this is no longer clearly marked, and fresh planting ahead may cause problems. I think it best that you travel south on the forest road, very overgrown at first, so don't be alarmed. Down through the forest, you will find it very damp underfoot at a clearing, but simply wade through. Exit through the second forestry gate to pass another sheep-dipping tank on your right. Turn right on surfaced road, passing the ruins of stone houses and, at a T-junction, where the surfaced road bears left, go right again. With the masts of Knockgour in your sights, you now face the final ascent. This is not quite as steep as it looks from afar. Put your head down, engage low gear and think of O'Sullivan Beara's winter walk — or of heaven, for on reaching the top, the view is heavenly. Northeast is Castletown Bearhaven. To the south is the tower on Black Ball Head, one of a string of sixteen built between 1804 and 1806 along the south coast from Youghal to Dursey. All were within view of one another, the intention being to communicate by semaphore or morse code. However, due to regular mists, the plan was not successful. Black Ball Head also featured on the introduction of steam railways, being proposed as a terminus in order to shorten the transatlantic journey by ship, a plan never pursued.

If you have the energy, you can detour to the three masts (TV/communications) on the summit of Knockgour (I assume *Cnoc Gabhar*, Hill of Goats). With or without detour, continue on the green road which is surfaced some two-thirds of the way down to the main road where you turn right for the nissen huts and village.

Distance: 15km/9.25miles. Ascent: 730m/2,400ft. Walking time: 5½ hours.

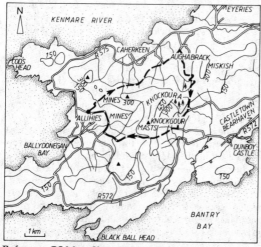

Reference OS Map: Sheet 24 (1:126,720).

6. GLANINCHIQUIN

A feature of the northwest facing side of the Beara Peninsula is the lake-filled glens carved into the mountains. Obviously, ice lasted longer and was more effective in scouring out coombes on northern slopes protected from the sun. A glen that might claim to be the most attractive is that containing Cloonee Loughs and Lough Inchiquin and our next walk gives plenty scope for enjoying it.

Turn off the R571/L62 (Tuosist-Kenmare) road at the signpost for Inchiquin Lakes. The drive of approximately 7km/4.5miles on the north shore of the lakes (right at the Y-junction of the surfaced roads), and ending in front of the waterfall (locally called the Cascade), sets the scene. Park your car at the end of the surfaced road (851 622) beyond the bridge. As I write, there is an honesty box (40p per person) hanging on the gate straight in front of the bridge for the use of visitors to the waterfall. You can enter there and after due contemplation, set a course southwest towards the spine leading up to point 483m/1,586ft known locally as Eskana (and shown on OS maps as Cummeenanimma). There is a clear line to the left of the spine. Underfoot, it is rocky and fern-covered with the result that the going is rough. However, the gain in height in a short time is spectacular. To the right of the spine as you travel upwards is the Robber's Den. Local tradition is that a robber was chased from this den and shot on the Bunane side of the hills. In the chase, he is said to have dropped a golden boot in the river pool beside your starting point.

By the time you reach the top of Eskana, there are views all around but you may decide to cross the turf banks to the cairn (or is it a small fallen sheep shelter?) at the top of Coomnadiha (645m/2,116ft) before taking a break for lunch. Glantrasna and Lauragh are below to the southwest. Beyond the Kenmare River, Scariff Island lies in the Atlantic beyond Lamb's Head. The Baurearagh Valley stretches to the northeast. But it is the view north and northwest that is most spectacular. In fact, this would be a perfect site for a lesson on the effects of the Ice Age. While Templenoe, centre of the ice cap which shaped much of the area, is not in view (it is east of the inlet of Sneem, clearly seen), the signs of the movement from there are obvious. You are looking north through the dramatic gash of the Gap of Dunloe carved out by the ice floe, while to the northwest is the Gap of Ballaghbeama, through which the ice moved to Caragh Lake and, beyond, Dingle Bay.

Immediately north of you is Cummeenadillure. Local tradition is that it was formerly *Coimin an Fhiolair* (Small Coombe of the Eagle). The eagle's nest was high above the lake which is 490m/1,600ft below you. The map is not clear but there is a mini-coombe above the main one and **this steep area must at all costs be avoided**. Taking a last look at Bantry Bay, set a course more or less directly east — the descent here is still a little steep but quite safe — towards the lake on the saddle below. As you descend, you can see clearly a sheep path leading from the lake north across the face of the ridge on your course. In good conditions, this is a good route but if wet, the lichen makes the rock slippery. It adds little to the journey to take the wide grassy slope leading from the lake to the right of the path. Either way, you reach the top of the saddle looking down into the Baurearagh Valley and can see how close the road comes at this point.

While it is possible to descend by the Cascade (to the north of the *Staca*, Stack), I suggest continuing north-northeast over Knocknagorraveela (*Cnoc na gCorra-mhiola*, Hill of Midges — none were in evidence while we were there) to follow the Maulagowna River. On the east bank of the river, you meet an almost complete ring ditch, possibly a cattle enclosure. Nearby are the traces of wide ridges, signs of tillage at a former settlement. A few ruins of stone houses still stand. There were apparently thirteen houses here and these may have been frame ones as there is a tradition that all neighbours gathered together to erect a 'cowluck' (very likely *cabhlach*, house frame) in a day. Look for the signs of the foundations of one house which seemingly never went beyond that stage.

The Maulagowna River joins the Glaninchiquin close to where you parked your car.

Distance: 9km/6miles. Ascent: 720m/2,350ft. Walking time: 4 hours.

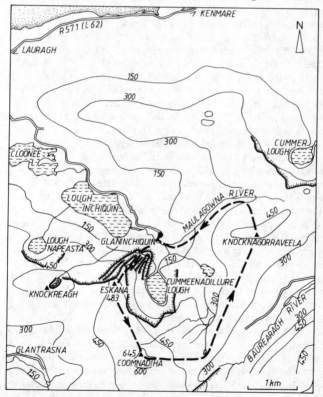

Reference OS Map: Killarney District (1:63,360).

7. CUMMEENGEERA

My favourite part of Beara is still that around Lauragh. The contrasts of rich wood, wild bog and mountain, lonely glen, lake, river and ever-present sea never fail to please. The distance from a centre of population adds to the attraction. The next walk gives a bird's-eye view of this wonderful land- and sea-scape while the walk in the glen described afterwards is a gentle introduction to the folk history of the area.

7(a) Cummeengeera Horseshoe

Travel less than 1km/0.5miles west of Lauragh School on the R571/L62 and take the road south, which leads to Glanmore Lake and Shronebirrane, for a short distance. (Incidentally, this walk can be shortened — see below.) After the small shop with a petrol pump, watch for two gates side by side on the right of the road on a slight left-hand bend. That on the right leads via the rhododendron avenue to a two-storey house which belongs to Denis O'Shea, a man well-versed in the history of the area. Approached with courtesy but, in deference to his age, not too early in the morning, Denis will not object to your travelling on the uphill path to the left of his house (763 575) which leads through a small wood (mainly holly) to open mountain beyond. Cross the wire fence ahead with care, and the ascent of the benches will quickly give views behind of Kilmakilloge Harbour with the renowned gardens of Dereen House at the inner end. To the left is the lower end of Glanmore Lake and across the slope above it, the ribbon of the Healy Pass Road. The views increase as you ascend to the top of Cummeennahillan (361m/1,183ft) where you can sit to study the rock structure exposed on the ridge, which runs from the north to the aptly named Knocknaveacal (*Cnoc na bhFiacal*, Hill of Teeth).

The undergrowth up to now has consisted of long grass, but crossing the saddle from Cummeennahillan, this changes to heather, dense in summer, which can be tiring. On a really hot day, I have succumbed and used the escape route left into the hanging valley from which one can zig-zag carefully to the right of the waterfall into Shronebirrane, the reverse of this being the alternative start suggested above (753 552). However, it is worth pushing on. After the molars of Knocknaveacal (514m/1,685ft) the heather disappears to allow quicker progress across turf and rock. The ridge runs from the 'Hill of Teeth' to Tooth Mountain (593m/1,945ft) but my practice has been to contour (traverse at the same level) on a direct line for Coomacloghane (600m/1,969ft), a rounded summit with many pools of water trapped on its rock shelves.

Now descend south to the saddle from which there is a short ascent to point 596m/1,956ft which again can be avoided by contouring (left). A view of Bantry Bay is now opening on your right while below on the left the Drimminboy River winds out of the valley towards the sea. The 601m/1,973ft peak which you pass over is shown on the map as Eskatarriff

(*Eisc a' Tairbh*, Steep Path of the Bull). This, properly speaking, is the name of one of the gullies leading down to the valley floor. You had passed another earlier called *Eisc na mBo* (Path of the Cows) — it leads down to the ruins of abandoned houses to be seen in the inner end of the valley.

Somewhere along the top of the cliffs on which you are now travelling, I recall on a still day producing a triple echo among the cliffs to the north and northwest, the second echo quite clear and the third just heard. Mindful of the friendly rivalry between the two counties and our position right on the border (represented by the dotted line on the OS map), one wit suggested that this was the Kerry method of throwing a Corkman's insult back in his face! On a later journey here, the wind foiled all attempts to produce even one echo.

From the next saddle, there is a stiff ascent to Lackabane (605m/1,984ft), known locally as Bullauns, and its twin peak, Curraghreague (600m/1,970ft), but this is rewarded by fresh views of Kilmakilloge Harbour ahead, the Glanmore Valley on the right, and behind you the inner end of Bantry Bay. A descent before the 380m/1,250ft shoulder beyond Curraghreague should not be attempted. From the shoulder, there is an escape route left — aim for the circular earthen fort from which a path leads to the surfaced road at Shronebirrane.

For those who wish to finish the ridge or to gain the Glanmore road, a route over Foilemon (known locally as Foilcannon) is possible but a course left is still essential. The wooded slope on the eastern side is very steep — it is said that when the trees were being planted, estate workers had to be lowered on to the benches by rope. There is a path east through the wood at the northern end of Glanmore Lake leading to the surfaced road.

Distance: 13.5km/8.5miles. Ascent: 760m/2,500ft. Walking time: 6 hours.

7(b) The Rabach's Glen

The walk on the valley floor into the hill-enclosed Cummeengeera (from local pronunciation, probably *Coimin gCaorach*, Sheep Pasture) would be a gentle respite after more serious walking and also suitable for a family group. Shortly after the surfaced road ends, park your car, with consideration, by the last houses in Shronebirrane (753 552) before the stone platform bridge. In a field on the right of the bungalow, you will see a stone circle, a record from pre-history, now a source of mystery to us. The path in the valley is quite clear at first, starting as a green road, crossing a stream and then left of the first rock outcrop which creates a narrow entrance. As the valley opens out, the path is not so distinct but there is an obvious line to the left under the steep slope of Bullauns (Lackabane on the OS map). The back of the valley is quite green and shows signs of fields and tillage. The Drimminboy River is now easily crossed to reach ruins which, while decayed, are good examples of simple stone dwellings in use in the last century. Surrounded by the towering rock walls of the

41

coombe, it is easy to imagine how hard it was to scrape a living here and why the area was eventually abandoned. No road ever reached this spot and the coffin of the last person to die in the valley had to be shouldered up to the road. Life was basic and the story of the Rabach must be viewed in that context.

Cornelius Sullivan *Rabach* (the word in Irish can mean 'violent' or 'vigorous', both of which seem appropriate) lived in one of these ruined dwellings, and locals claim him to be the last man hanged in Munster, in 1831. It seems that a sailor (probably a deserter from the British Navy base on Beara Island, directly south across the hills) arrived at the house, seek-ing lodgings for the night. Urged on by his father (the Old Rabach), Con murdered the sailor in the belief that he had money. The body was hidden under the hearth stone. A woman neighbour who had risen early to go   to the well for fresh water for tea (her husband was a horseman who regularly made the two-day journey to the Cork Butter Exchange, trading his own and neighbour's butter for other provisions) saw the deed through the window but kept silence at the time. During a dispute, she was unfortunate enough to tell the Rabach that she had information that could 'put him away for good'. On her next visit to the hill to tend cows, the Rabach followed her, strangled her with a spancel and left her, head down, in a stream to simulate drowning. This was in 1814. No one else apparently knew of these events until a man, injured in the Allihies mines, confessed on his deathbed in 1830 that he had been on the hill (stealing cows' tails, then a reprehensible crime) and had seen the second murder. The chase was then on, but the Rabach evaded capture by making use of a den in the rocks still known as *Pluais an Rabach*.

The Pluais is above the house to the northwest. The Rabach resorted to the den only in times of danger and he easily outran police sent for him (it is said that an autopsy revealed that he had a double heart). In January 1831, the dead woman's son, who had only been a year old at her death, alerted the police that the Rabach would be at home for the birth of a child and they availed of the opportunity to make their capture. Despite its his-tory, the glen is today a haven of peace. Having sampled that peace and the atmosphere of the glen, you can return by the route you came.

Distance: 3.5km/2.25miles. Ascent: 110m/350ft. Walking time: 1½ hours.

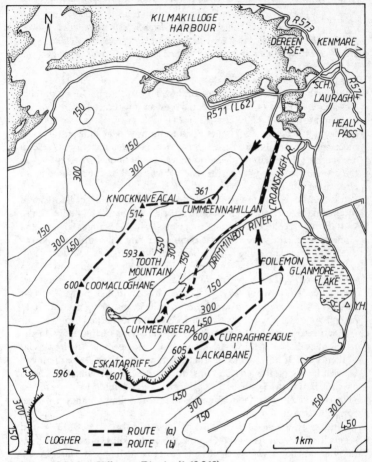

Reference OS Map: Killarney District (1:63,360).

8. BUNANE-GLANMORE

There are a number of walks which can be used for the journey from Bunane Youth Hostel to that in Glanmore as a follow-up to Walk 2. The first, described below, takes you over the remainder of the Caha Mountains and after that, a number of lower-level alternatives, partly along roads, are suggested.

8(a) Over the Hills

From the hostel, cross the Bunane Bridge and travel uphill along the surfaced road to Esk from where what is now an (unsurfaced) forestry road leads to the 358m/1,174ft pass (926 606) — this presumably was the road to Glengarriff before the Tunnel Road to the west was built in the early nineteenth century. From the pass, travel over Esk Mountain (388m/1,275ft) and Turners Rock (425m/1,393ft) to cross the roof of the highest tunnel on the present Kenmare-Glengarriff road, which could have been used as an alternative route to reach this point.

At this stage, my approach would be to contour south of Baurearagh Mountain (490m/1,607ft) on a bearing direct for Killane Mountain (523m/1,716ft). My recollection of this ridge between the Baurearagh and the Upper Glengarriff valleys is that there are many short ups and downs until you reach the ridge coming in from the right to create the 592m/1,941ft saddle to the southeast of the peaks of Caha and Eagles Nest, which are bypassed. You are now truly in the Caha Mountains (*ceathach*, showery) and I hope that for your sake, they do not live up to their name. Descend then, via the lake, to Ram's Hill (527m/1,728ft) and along the saddle to ascend the rocky Knockeirky (581m/1,906ft) with its cairned top.

Up to now, you have been enjoying variations of the views in the previous walk but at Knockeirky, new vistas are opening. The lower end of Bantry Bay is now sighted and as you continue, Adrigole Harbour can be seen below on the left. On the saddle between Cushnaficulla (*Cois na bhFiacla*, Beside the Teeth) and Knockowen, the rock folds are more or less with you. Perched on the rock seams are many solitary boulders — presumably Ice Age deposits.

Sitting by the small cairn on Knockowen (661m/2,169ft), the world seems to be at your feet. Who Owen was I do not know but if he sat here, his viewing point was well picked. Adrigole Valley and Harbour are below on the left. Glanmore Valley and Kilmakilloge Harbour are on the right, and ahead are Hungry Hill and the rest of the ocean-fringed Beara Peninsula. From Knockowen, there is a clear ridge over Claddaghgarriff (possibly *Cladrach Garbh*, Rough Rock-Strewn Place) to the 329m/1,081ft top of the Healy Pass, which is also the meeting place of the Cork-Kerry border, a point significant to the following tradition.

The road over the pass was not completed until the 1930s. Before that, there was a road 3km/2miles into the glen from Adrigole and a similar situation on the northern side of the pass. Two paths were in use — one for pedestrians and the other, known as *Eisc na gCorp* (Steep Path of the Bodies), used for funerals. The conduct of some of these funerals is fascinating. In the last century, it was apparently the practice, not confined to this area, that if a wife died childless, she was not buried with her husband's people but her body was sent to her former parish. Thus, if a woman from Lauragh married in Adrigole and died without issue, her body was taken for burial in Lauragh via *Eisc na gCorp*. It was the responsibility of the Corkmen to shoulder the coffin as far as the top where there was a flat rock. Here they received from the Kerrymen meeting them the instruction, *Cuir anuas ansin e* (Place it down there). However, there was a belief that if the coffin could be pushed one foot into the Kerry side, the Corkmen could rid themselves of bad luck. Needless to say, the Kerrymen declined this dubious gift and it seems that the resulting battles were often furious! The Eisc is a clear wide gully some distance behind the seasonal shop near the top known as Don's Cabin, and the rock (a pear-shaped one) can still be pointed out.

The pedestrian path comes up from the south on the eastern side of the road and crosses it from east to west on the Glanmore side just below a large rock after the first U-bend. In fact, the path down to the youth hostel (still marked as a school on some maps) is not now complete. The going is dry, however, and it is easy to make a descent on the course of the dotted line on the map, enjoying in the meantime the views of Glanmore, the wood of Dereen House and the sea beyond.

Distance: 18.5km/11.5miles. Ascent: 860m/2,800ft. Walking time: 7 hours.

8(b) By Road and Hill

A number of possibilities exist for creating low-level long-distance walks in Beara and I outline some in case you wish to remain off traffic-ridden roads without resorting to high ground.

The first alternative is to leave the hostel, travel along the main Kenmare-Glengarriff road for about 2km/1mile and then turn right at Releagh Bridge to take the road uphill (right again at the Y-junction) over the 236m/774ft pass and down to the Dromoughty River valley to join the Kenmare-Lauragh Road. This still leaves a long distance along a main road but nevertheless a road which offers much in the way of scenery.

Perhaps a better choice would be to go left at the Y-junction to follow the road into the Baurearagh Valley. This road ends very close to the top of the saddle northeast of Coomnadiha, from where you could follow the second half of Walk 6 and go through the most attractive Glaninchiquin Valley. From here, the walk on the main road is a relatively short one over the saddle at Garrane and down to wooded Lauragh, and then there is a choice of roads into Glanmore.

Use of the main road can be avoided for longer by leaving the Baurearagh Valley to ascend Baurearagh Mountain and following the course of Walk 8(a) as far as Ram's Hill. From here, there is a descent west into the Glanrastel Valley. A disused road on the southern side of that valley (a dotted line on some OS maps) takes you out at Lauragh, about 5km/3miles from the hostel. The Glanrastel Valley, like all of Beara, is steeped in history. It is said that 'Mysterious Number One', one of the Invincibles involved in the Phoenix Park Murders (1882) stayed here — in one of the houses on the southern road I suggest you follow — before being taken by boat to America from Bantry Bay. Southeast of Shinnagh (the placename must be *sionnach*, fox), deep in the pocket, is *Pluais Carraig na Scriob* (Den of the Rock of Writings), a slab of rock leaning against another to form a den, the upright wall inscribed for its full length. The impression was of prehistoric writings in a language not yet deciphered. However, an inspection showed series of straight lines which might have been made by the bayonets of Whiteboys (scourge of landlords and agents in the 1760s) in hiding.

No time or distance is given for the alternatives nor is a sketch map included as they are meant for those who can plot the details of a route for themselves. They should be regarded as all-day walks. One word of warning — I have found that the names shown on the OS map for hill and mountain tops in Beara are not those in everyday use by sheep farmers and others who frequent the higher ground. For that reason, care should be taken to make yourself clear if seeking directions or information.

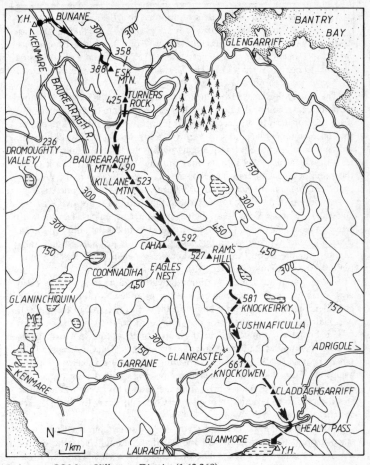

Reference OS Map: Killarney District (1:63,360).

9. THE PAPS

From wherever they are seen, whether from the N22 (Ballyvourney-Killarney/County Boundary road) or the N72 (Rathmore-Killarney road) or from other summits, it is clear why The Paps (Da Chioch Dhana, Two Breasts of Dana or Anu) received their name. The twin rounded summits surmounted by two cairns provide easy climbing and — due to their relatively isolated position — views over amazingly long distances.

The usual approach is from the top of the green road (143 852) running along the east side of the East Pap. It is quite possible to drive to the top from the northern (Rathmore) side but if approaching from Clonkeen on the south, you may have to park your car below the top and walk up. This pass is known as the *Sloigeadal*, a quagmire or quicksand — inappropriate for so rocky a place. Set into the midst of the rock and scree is a lake, on the map Lough Glannafreaghaun (*Gleann na Fraochan*, Valley of the Whortleberry or Hurt) a name not now in use. Locals refer to it as Shrone Lake.

At the top of the pass, to the west of the road, there are two wired-in enclosures planted with trees. Between them runs a passageway with wire 'gates' at both ends. Lift the wire loop to untie the gates and close them after use. Once through the passageway, it is just a question of zig-zagging up the slope through heather, interspersed with the tiny hurt plant, to the East Pap (696m/2,284ft).

There, you find a massive mound over 6m/20ft high with a cairn 3m/10ft high on it. It is believed that the mound is a prehistoric burial chamber. Signs of prehistoric pagan fertility rites abound in this area. It was claimed that Munster owed its prosperity to the Goddess Anu on whose breast we stand, and to the north of the peak, in Gortnagane, where a Penitential Station is shown on the map, is 'The City', a stone fort where rounds (walking in a circle reciting prayers) of a well were made each May Day. It was thought to have been associated with one of the sisters of Anu but given a Christian aspect later. Until very recent times, sick animals were brought from all over Cork and Kerry to 'The City' for the cure available at the well.

From the east peak, descend to the saddle over Commeen (the very steep ground to the north) with the Pap Lake, Lough Nageeha on the map, in its centre. The green line of a sheep path which runs up from Gortacareen can be seen coming in on your right — it could have been used as an alternative approach to this point. Ascend 90m/300ft or so beside the upright stones called the Fiacla (Teeth) to the top of the West Pap (693m/2,273ft). The mound and cairn here are not as grand but the ruined chamber entrance can be seen. The views from the east summit are surpassed here. Only haze or cloud will prevent you from enjoying a panorama from Kenmare Bay to Dingle Bay and beyond to the west and to the north, east and south; the views from this point are almost unlimited.

The return journey is as you came. When you reach Shrone Lake, it might be worth looking for a rock which I am told lies over the lake on the line of a path which ran on its western side before the green road was made. The story is told that a man had the audacity to steal a bull from among the hundreds of animals gathered at 'The City' below for the May Day. He took it across Sloigeadal to Ballyvourney but was traced there through the imprint left on the solid rock. The representation of the nails of his boot, the ferrule of his stick and the hoofmarks of the bull are still as clear 'as if he had walked on liquid concrete'. Not having visited it, I cannot give precise directions but a local should be able to guide you if you are determined to inspect it.

Distance: 4km/2.5miles. Ascent: 580m/1,900ft. Walking time: 2½ hours.

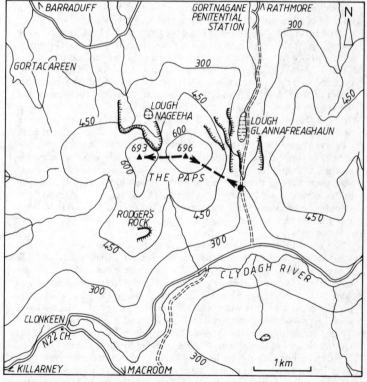

Reference OS Map: Sheet 21 (1:126,720).

10. BENNAUNMORE-CAPPAGH

Our first walk in the Killarney district is a short one into the centre of one of the few areas of volcanic activity. The walk would be very suitable for shorter days and in fact, as explained later, there may be advantages in travelling in winter.

Approaching either off the N22 (Cork-Killarney Road) or the N71 (Killarney-Kenmare Road), take the road which travels along the east side of Lough Guitane, through gates. It might be as well to park your car at the open ground near the end of the lake (034 839) and walk (left) as far as the red-roofed disused house. From there, follow the course of the stream coming down from the outcrop west of Crohane which is the 659m/ 2,162ft peak to the left ahead. The ground on this part of the walk is covered with orange-tinted sundew. There is a path of sorts, at first to the left of the stream, later on the right. In places, it seems to be built up and this may be the line of the old path to Kilgarvan. In fact, as you round the higher ground on the right, you arrive at a boggy plateau which has a number of stone uprights which might also have marked the route.

The first of the two secluded lakes snuggled in this long narrow valley 300m/1,000ft above sea level is now ahead of you. This is Lough Nabroda, sitting below the volcanic columns of Bennaunmore, claimed to be the Giant's Causeway of Kerry. The north-flowing stream out of the lake runs underground through scree fall. Following the path on the east side of the lake and across the boggy saddle between, you arrive on the west side of the second lake — Crohane Lake (sometimes known as *Loch Carraigh a' Beithe*, Lake of the Rock of the Birch Tree). There could be no greater contrast than the setting of these lakes — a microcosm of mountain scenery. Where the first lake sits below steep scree-covered slopes, the second is among more rounded ground, richly carpeted with purple heather, at least in summer. The path is somewhat clearer here and by its side, you will see a flat stone carved with names and initials. J. C. Coleman in his classic *The Mountains of Killarney* (1948) refers to a carved ice-smoothed rock beside the obvious big crag but I could not find it. My visit was in high summer and features may be clearer when the undergrowth is not as thick.

At the southern end of Crohane Lake, there are fine views south and southeast to Morley's Bridge and into the Roughty River valley. In Walk 1, we had been looking at that valley from the other end and we are now likely to be on the earlier part of the Pilgrims' route on their way to honour St Finbarr on Gougane Sunday. It is remarkable what great travellers our ancestors were before the motor car. In the Gougane Barra area, I was told that groups still make the annual trip (a longer one now by car) each August to the three-day Puck Fair in Killorglin, lying to the west of us and at least 70km/40miles even by this route from Gougane. They are continuing the tradition of their predecessors who must have travelled here on foot or on horseback or perhaps droving animals.

Travel right now to rise up to the 300m/1,000ft level and arrive over the wooded Cappagh valley. *Ceapach* can mean a decayed or denuded wood — appropriate in this case. There is a nonsense phrase in use in Killarney, apparently connected with the place. When asked where he is going, rather than give a direct answer, a person may respond 'To Cappagh for a load of hake'. From where you stand, there is the impression of a steep drop to the valley floor below, which however is only 200m/700ft or so under you — the impression is due to the narrowness of the valley. Nevertheless, it is best to avoid the steep descent by travelling north along the ridge to the saddle before the peak of Bennaunmore (454m/1,490ft) a variant of *Beann Mor*, Big Peak. From there, you can with a little care descend the less steep slope to meet the edge of what has been termed a petrified forest. This description would be most merited in winter when the bare trees create a phantom scene.

There is now a pleasant evening stroll out of the glen between the towering slabs of Bennaunmore and the Cappagh River. This valley is lower than that to the east and much richer in vegetation. There are more trees — even if they are small — than we usually associate with hill walks in Ireland. After the narrower rockier gorge, you meet at the north end of Bennaunmore a 'scar' of a road which leads to the red-roofed house which was your starting point.

Distance: 8km/5miles. Ascent: 490m/1,600ft. Walking time: 3½ hours.

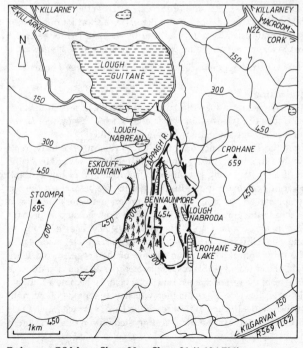

Reference OS Maps: Sheet 20 or Sheet 21 (1:126,720).

11. MANGERTON

While Mangerton (840m/2,756ft) is dealt with in greater detail in the circuit of the Horses' Glen (Walk 12), there are other approaches through the National Park giving quicker and easier access to the vantage point which the summit provides. Two are described below.

11(a) The Tooreencormick Bridle Path

This provides the most gradual ascent. Near Muckross on the N71/T65, take the road left signposted 'Mangerton Viewing Park' and at the upper end of the wood, swing right. Pass the car park and continue to the end of the surfaced road to park by a concrete bridge.

From here (983 848), a path once used as a tourist pony route runs uphill. Initially, it crosses a stream and the Finoulagh River and continues up on the eastern side of that river. On your right is the site of a battle in 1262 in which the McCarthys defeated the Normans. In the battle, Cormac McCarthy fell, thus giving his name to the place. The path shortly swings right to meet an estate boundary fence which runs (left) directly up to the Devil's Punch Bowl. Just before the lake is a small beehive stone shelter, once used by estate gamekeepers.

Go uphill along the north side of the lake to cross the arête between the Punch Bowl and Glenacappul. From there, it is a short journey south-west to the summit cairn. You can descend by the southern edge of the Punch Bowl to rejoin the path at the Bachelor's Well and thus homeward.

Distance: 9.5km/6miles. Ascent: 700m/2,300ft. Walking time: 4 hours.

11(b) By Foilacurrane

As an alternative, you can take the much more scenic approach through the shaded slopes of Muckross Forest. The walk is not as gradual as the previous one and at one stage involves some scrambling.

Start from the Torc car park on the N71/T65 Killarney-Kenmare road and follow the attractive tourist footpath up beside the waterfall. At the upper end of the path, swing left on the forest road and continue uphill along the various roads (or more directly via the fire-breaks). At the top end of the upper road, go uphill beside the stream and across the stile on the forest fence to the gorge ahead. This is shown on the map as Barnan-currane (*Bearna an Corrain*, Gap of the Sickle) usually known locally as Foilacurrane (*faill*, cliff). The gorge is a fairly steep scramble, made easier now by the provision of steps. From the top of the gorge, an old fence runs straight ahead (east) — this once separated the tenants' commonage (to the south) from the rest of the demesne, long before it became a National Park. Follow the fence to meet another which you should follow right uphill (now beside the Bridle Path) to reach the Devil's Punch Bowl. Once again, a clockwise circuit of the Bowl is suggested but on this occasion, if you travel directly west from the summit of Mangerton, you will meet the western peak, on some OS maps showing the 725m/2,379ft point. The cairn marked on the map is in fact a natural rock outcrop.

Here you are looking down on the Owengarriff River which feeds Torc Waterfall. Take the line of your choice down to cross the river (provided it is not in flood, of course) and join the Old Kenmare Road which runs down on the western side of the river and across a bridge (right) to meet the path by which you ascended. On this course, you are almost certain to observe deer, either the native Irish red deer or the imported Japanese sika, which frequent the area — the higher ground in the summer and lower down in winter.

Distance: 11km/7miles. Ascent: 800m/2,650ft. Walking time: 4¾ hours.

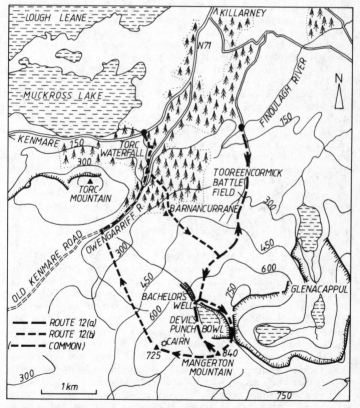

Reference OS Map: Killarney National Park (1:25,000).

↑

A fine day's walking coupled with magnificent views and a well-illustrated lesson in geology is provided by the horseshoe around Glenacappul (Gleann na gCapall, *Horses' Glen*).

If approaching from Muckross off the N71/T65, after the Owgarriff Bridge take the road right, on the western side of Lough Guitane, and almost immediately park near the next bend where there is an open space with a bridge leading to two gated bohereens (005 855). If approaching from Glenflesk off the N22/T29, turn left at the Y-junction after the Finow Bridge to arrive at the same spot. Cross the bridge and enter the left gate (ensure it and all other gates are closed after you) to follow the bohereen for over a mile (leaving one house on the left and another at the end on the right). If your walk is in late spring, the furze creates a riot of yellow flower in contrast to the rocky morainic pile which lines the bohereen to the right. From the second house, go left on a grassy path, through the gate in the wire fence and then follow the west bank of the well-named Owgarriff (*Abhann Garbh*, Rough River) to cross to the east on a wooden bridge where it leaves Lough Garagarry.

Now, rise up on the shoulder ahead to the double top of Stoompa, the higher one (695m/2,281ft) with a cairn. As you ascend, the terraced nature of the floor of the Horses' Glen becomes clear. From the path, looking back, the town and the Lower Lake of Killarney are laid out for you. On the left is the pointed Bennaunmore and, beyond, the obvious twin summits of The Paps. Bennaunmore was, of course, the source of the volcanic rock thrown as far as Mangerton and this was the reason why these coombes — before Ice Age effects were understood — were thought to be extinct volcanoes. Descend to the turf banks of the saddle before ascending above the steep walls towards Mangerton. It is on this stretch that, due to its L shape, you see for the first time the complete glen with massive rock walls carved out to enclose the three lakes — Lough Garagarry, Lough Managh and Lough Erhogh. These are termed paternoster lakes due to the similarity to prayer beads and, typically, each one is at a lower level than the one inside it.

The 840m/2,756ft top of Mangerton (*Mong-phortach*, Long-grassed Bog) is very rounded — it stood above the ice which carved out the coombes — with many turf banks, now eroded in places by the weather down to the gravel beneath and dotted with a number of water pools. The actual summit is marked by a small cairn which could be missed — look for the single upright stone which sticks up from its centre and which first comes into view. Latterly, an OS triangulation pillar has stood here but these are being removed from some summits.

One of perhaps the earliest travellers to Killarney, Isaac Weld Esq. MRIA, described his experience on this summit in his *Illustrations of the Scenery of Killarney and the Surrounding Country* (1812):

I was once with a party which had been shooting on the mountains beyond Mangerton, and, on the way back to Killarney, had to cross this plain. On advancing, the air became obscure; and, at last, such dense vapours enveloped us, that it was impossible to distinguish an object at the distance of a few yards. Under these circumstances we continued to walk, for more than two hours, over an unvaried surface, where no track whatsoever was visible; our guide still asserting that he was leading us home by the shortest possible route. The mist soon penetrated our clothes, and we began to experience all the inconvenience of wet and cold, when the guide, suddenly stopping, took off his coat, turned it inside out, and again deliberately put it on. We marvelled very much at this extraordinary proceeding, and his reluctance to give a satisfactory reply to our inquiries into the motives of it, served but to excite still greater curiosity. At last, being pressed for an explanation, he acknowledged that he was totally ignorant of our situation, and had turned his coat as a charm of potent influence to enable a lost man to recover his way. The intelligence was unwelcome: the day was fast approaching to a close, and there was danger of our taking the very opposite course to that which ought to be followed.

After many escapades, fulsomely described, the party ended up in Cappagh. The same gentleman was again unfortunate in the choice of guide to take him up Carrauntuohill (or Gheraun-tuel as he terms it) — an adventurous trip ended with the realisation that they had been led up and down the wrong mountain!

In case you are also in doubt, look for an arrow made from a series of stones laid in line which has for many years pointed more or less north to take you to the edge of the steep slope down to the Devil's Punch Bowl from where the arête on the right is clearly seen. Given the right day, this narrow ridge is a fine spot to sit for a bite and a view. Three lakes (to the east the upper two in the Horses' Glen and to the west the Devil's Punch Bowl) are in sight — four, in fact, if you allow for the Lower Killarney Lake which lies to the northwest with Dingle Bay and the mountains of Corkaguiney beyond.

Incidentally, if fog has overtaken you, I suggest going west or northwest. There is a fairly wide path contouring along the west slope of Mangerton, said to be the continuation of the bridle path coming from the north and intended to circle around to the summit, which will act as a kind of handrail and can be followed north to meet the outlet of the Devil's Punch Bowl, marked Bachelor's Well on the map.

From the arête, sheep tracks lead along the left of the unnamed peak to the north — J. C. Coleman calls it Mangerton North. From there, the line is clear down to the wooden bridge at the outlet of Lough Garagarry.

Distance: 15km/9.5miles. Ascent: 1,040m/3,400ft. Walking time: 6½ hours.

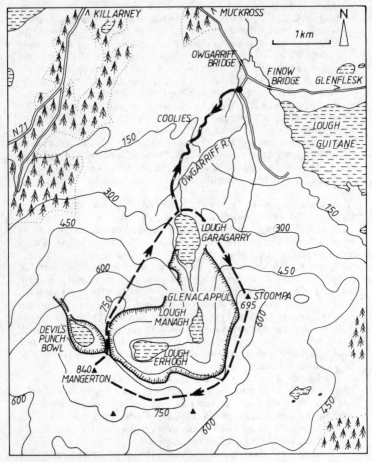

Reference OS Maps: Sheet 20 or Sheet 21 (1:126,720).

The first leg of the Kerry Way takes you through the Killarney National Park, sampling history and nature, and into the isolated Black Valley.

Take the N71/T65 (Kenmare road) from Killarney town (96 90). 2km/ 1.25miles from the Flesk Bridge is the first entrance on the right to Killarney National Park. Follow the roadway beside Lough Leane (*Loch Lein*, Lake of Learning — a reference to the Early Christian university on Innisfallen Island). If you are intent on completing the Kerry Way, pass by the detour (left after 0.8km/0.5miles) to the ruins of Muckross Abbey (*Muc-ros*, Wooded Promontory of the Pig). The history and attractions of the National Park and of Muckross House and Gardens, which require a separate visit, are outlined in special publications available at the House. After 1.6km/1mile, the lakeside road splits. Follow the sign left for the House and Torc Waterfall and then continue past the House onto the roadway skirting Muckross Lake. This meets the Owengarriff River (*Abhann Garbh*, Rough River). The placenames, Muckross and Torc (*torc*, boar), lead to the belief that swine were the main occupants of this area in early times. The most famous present-day residents are the deer — the only surviving herd of pure Irish red deer and the Japanese sika. Concern for preservation of the deer dictates that large numbers of people do not press on deeply into the Park and the marked routes answer that wish. The path goes under the N71 and up beside the Waterfall, a strenuous walk but with viewing platforms giving excuse for a rest. Go right over the stone bridge and then left with the forest walk sign on the track which runs southwest above the river. A detour to viewing platforms on the western face of Torc Mountain is possible by taking the second path right — this being the intended route of the Kerry Way but abandoned by the Park authorities because it led to long stretches along the busy N71.

With the Owengarriff below you on the left, disregard the road left and continue straight through the gateway with low stone pillars. A little later, go through the timber forest gate onto open mountain. The cobbled nature underfoot suggests that this is an old road. In fact, it is the Old Kenmare Road, closed during the Clearances when tenants were evicted to permit 'development' of estates. Passage to America, very often on coffin ships, was paid by some landlords. Mangerton Mountain is up on the left with the field system of Ferta underneath. Torc Mountain rises on the right. Follow the road over two saddles with views right of the MacGilly-cuddy's Reeks and descend to the track through soft ground, mercifully fitted by National Park staff with short log footbridges. It seems as I write that a gravelled path is being added. At any rate, the path leads you across the Crinnagh River under Coars Waterfall with its pleasant pool. By the time you walk, the path may be more defined (this area has been out of use as, understandably, the members of the Kerry Deer Society have reservations about even serious walkers causing disturbance) but if not, aim for the trees and rock outcrops of Esknamucky Glen (*Eisc na Muice*, Narrow Gorge of the Pigs). The tinkling stream under the shade of remnants of old oak wood might tempt you to linger. The walking route continues across bog which can be quite wet at any time of year. Maintain a straight line southwest to meet the (red rust) zinc roof and stone sheep pen and begin the descent to more extensive woodland, crossing the Galway's River by footbridge. The route winds through the wood and loops west before meeting surfaced road. If your intention is to complete the full circuit of the Kerry Way, note this point. On the return walk from Kenmare, you will arrive back here.

To reach the Black Valley, turn right now over two stone bridges and meet the N71 at the former Derrycunnihy church. Continue straight past the church for about 20m/yds and take the track right descending through a wood. (There may be a temporary winter detour to protect the feeding grounds of the Greenland white-fronted goose. If so, it will be signposted.) The permanent path descends on the left side of the Galway's River to the site of Queen's Cottage. This was built especially for the visit of Queen Victoria in August 1861 so that Her Majesty could have afternoon tea in comfort. It commanded a view of Derrycunnihy Cascade which you have just passed. The cottage, demolished in 1921, stood on the green between the wooden footbridge which leads right to the N71 and the existing ruin — Dotie's Cottage, named for the last resident, herdsman 'Dotie' O'Donoghue.

Turn left through Derrycunnihy (*Doire Caithne*, Oakwood of the Arbutus Tree), following a Mass Path which led from the Black Valley to the church above. The tradition was that the men walked along your route ahead while the women were ferried by boat. This area is one of the few remaining examples of ancient Irish oak woods. Typically, in sandstone ground, holly trees and bushes form the understorey. Proof of the purity of the air is the prolific growth of lichen and mosses on tree limbs. This is also a place to observe two species of Lusitanian plants unique to the area. The plants are natives of the Mediterranean but flourish in the mild wet climate of the southwest. Killarney is associated with the largest specimen, *arbutus unedo*, the arbutus/strawberry tree. The second is the Irish spurge, *euphorbia hyberna*, a poisonous plant once sought by poachers. As you leave the wood, and still on the lakeshore, a look back northwest to Torc Mountain shows how far you have come. The path now leads through open bogland. In wet weather, avoid the higher path over the rocks — the lichen may be dangerously slippy underfoot. In the bog, look for but do not pick the light green star-fish shaped great butterwort (*pinguicula grandiflora*). The flower, seen in early summer, resembles a violet, both in shape and colour. The plant is extremely rare outside of Kerry and it is carniverous, compensating for the lack of minerals in the acid bog by trapping and digesting insects which are always visible on the green leaf. Having passed on your left the turf bank where peat is cut for fuel, look for the hurt/whortleberry growing underfoot in profusion. Through a gate (please close it) and over a footbridge, pass the boat channel and it is time for a rest.

Lord Brandon's Cottage is a welcome refreshment stop. While the season is Easter and mid-May to September, light refreshments are available throughout the year from the ever-helpful Mr and Mrs Michael O'Connor. Boats ply between here and Ross Castle in Killarney in season. The last boat leaves for Ross at 2.30 p.m. but Mr O'Connor is willing always to take a latecomer across the lake to the N71 in his own boat. This is the site of Lord Brandon's shooting lodge. He was one of the Crosbies of Ardfert, and he unexpectedly succeeded to his cousin's title and was able to indulge his passion for shooting. The cottage itself no longer stands but the stone tower, used to watch for poachers, and the old house, once stables on the ground floor and groom's accommodation overhead, remain.

Cross the bridge and turn left beside the Gearhameen River (*Gaortha Min*, smooth woodland) up the roadway which leads to the Roman Catholic church and the Black Valley Youth Hostel. This could be a useful overnight stop but be warned, advance booking is recommended both for the hostel and other accommodation. Purple Mountain rises to your right. In certain lights, particularly near sunset, the red sandstone scree allows the mountain to live up to its name. As you proceed towards the hostel, the full might of the MacGillycuddy's Reeks is clear ahead.

Distance: 23km/14.25miles (longer if a winter detour is in use — check at the Tourist Office). Ascent: 400m/1,300ft. Walking time: 6¾ hours.

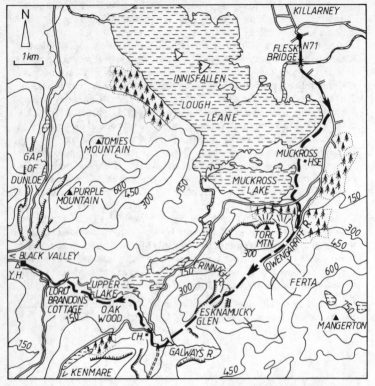

Reference Maps: OS Killarney National Park (1:25,000) or Kerry Way Map Guide (1:50,000).

14. TORC MOUNTAIN

For someone seeking a relatively short walk in the Killarney area offering a good viewing point, Torc Mountain (Torc, Wild Boar) provides the answer.

You can walk from Killarney as for Walk 13 or take your car to the car park on the N71/T65 at the bottom of Torc Waterfall (965 847). Ascend by the cascade and continue onto open mountain on the Old Kenmare Road. Stay on the road until you are level with the point where the Owengarriff River swings away southeast. You can swing more or less north and begin your ascent here. There is a bridle path which can only be discerned in places. However, your line ahead is clear — aim for the shoulder to the left of the peak. In the later stages, short rock faces cross your path. These force you to zig-zag, the correct thing to do on any ascent.

As you climb, take time to look behind. The area around Cores Hill shows many signs of former habitation — walls, old tillage, etc. In fact, if you had continued further along the Old Kenmare Road, you would have seen a number of ruined houses. These were inhabited until the Clearances — a period when many landlords felt that open land for deer hunting was more important than the resident tenants, who were simply evicted. It was at that stage that the present Killarney-Kenmare Road was built, as the bridges on the Old Road were knocked down to prevent public passage. Behind Cores Hill and between the two branches of the Upper Crinnagh River lies *Inse Baile na mBo* (Inch of the Town of the Cows), presumably the site of a booley village, that is, one inhabited only in the summer when cattle were taken to the higher grazing land.

As you climb, the Upper Killarney Lake comes into view over the shoulder to the left with the sugarloaf of Broaghnabinnia behind it and to the right of that the ridge of the MacGillycuddy's Reeks. The knife edge of Cummeenapeasta, the centre section of that ridge walk, is clearly seen.

At the top of Torc (535m/1,764ft), all three Killarney Lakes are in view. To the right is Lough Guitane and to the left Looscaunagh Lough. The sea — the inner end of Dingle Bay — is also to be seen. In fact, a look at the map will show how well situated Torc is as a viewing place — it pro-trudes out over the lakes from the centre of a crescent created by the peaks of the National Park.

Your descent should be by the course you ascended. However tempting it may seem as a short cut to the bridge, going down by the east side of Torc would be very foolhardy. Keep a keen eye out for deer, usually seen in this area.

Distance: 9.5km/6miles. Ascent: 530m/1,750ft. Walking time: 3¾ hours.

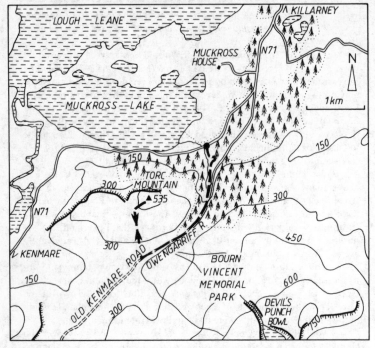

Reference OS Map: Killarney National Park (1:25,000).

15. PURPLE MOUNTAIN

The Purple Mountain range on the west side of Lough Leane provides very good climbing and viewing points. It can be approached from a number of directions but I am using a south-north attack which would be suitable for anyone leaving the Black Valley Youth Hostel.

From near the turn of the road over the youth hostel (871 833), follow the line of a stream and fence, northeast. A rock wall is on the right and where, after some distance, the stream swings left towards its face, continue with the fence as far as Glas Lough. For some reason, this lake always seems to be nearer the start than expected — a good complaint. It provides a good point to rest for a bite and a view — south over the peaks of Iveragh, southwest into lake-strewn Cummeenduff (the Black Valley) and west down into the ice-carved gorge of the Gap of Dunloe.

At the end of the lake, a heather-clad slope commences and runs up to the right. In fact, the fence conveniently continues on our course for a while. Follow it to the end, from where you bear slightly left to rise to the summit. This slope satisfies one's notions of what a mountain should be like — a fairly steep rock and scree-covered slope. The sandstone of which the Reeks are made is of various hues and here the rock is definitely purple. Viewed from a distance, in a certain light, this is more distinct. On the ascent, you meet a number of cairns. I judge the fourth heap of stones — really a small circle — to be the peak top (832m/2,739ft). As might be expected, the vistas have expanded.

At the summit, there is a sense of being on the roof of the world. This is the effect of a clear ridge stretching north over the sheer drop on the right. Generally, particularly at the start, there are sheep tracks and one is encouraged to bound along towards Tomies. At the 'complex junction', where the ridge from Shehy Mountain on the east enters, there is a risk of going astray in fog. If this should happen to you, the one thing that must not be done is to go west into the Gap. Almost any other course is safe.

At any rate, there is little point in being here without views. At the junction, you must decide whether to travel east to Shehy Mountain (571m/1,827ft), claimed to be the one vantage point commanding all three Killarney Lakes.

If you are not doing so, continue on to the turf saddle leading to the summit of Tomies (735m/2,413ft). The mounds of stones here are said to mark burial places. Dingle Bay is now seen to the northwest across the plain of mid-Kerry. Across the Gap from you, zig-zagging towards the bare trees on the hill edge, is the track which is the beginning of the Reeks Ridge Walk. Your course ahead is north-northwest (a detour to Tomies Rock is optional) down the heather slope to the L in the river near Kate Kearney's Cottage. Approaching this, I suggest that you continue to the end of the spur, beyond the river, and then swing back on the path leading out beside it to the surfaced road.

Distance: 8km/5miles. Ascent: 700m/2,300ft. Walking time: 4 hours (please note that this walking time does not include returning through the Gap to the Black Valley which will take another 2 hours).

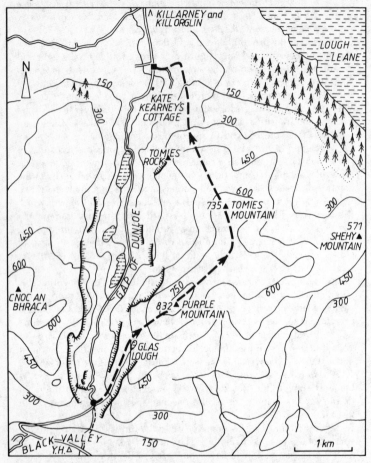

Reference OS Maps: Killarney National Parks or MacGillycuddy's Reeks (1:25,000).

16. TOMIES

This peak has already been included in the previous walk. However, for someone seeking a shorter outing, it is worth doing on its own, particularly for the walk down through the Gortdirra Valley at close of day.

The first part of the walk is a reverse of the end of the Purple Mountain course. Start at the road going east from the surfaced road (882 892) to the north of the bridge north of Kate Kearney's Cottage (the car park opposite 'the Cottage' can be used). Pass through two gates, the second at the end of the surfaced road, and keep straight on the path which swings left to the end of the spur. This leads up, south-southeast, to the stony top of Tomies (733m/2,413ft). From there, you can continue on the ridge top towards the 762m/2,503ft point. Unless intending to include Shehy Mountain, take the line of your choice down through Gortdirra, always known locally as Coomcloghane. The views over the lake and the rich variety of trees make this a very pleasurable descent. On the way, you pass some ruins which may be those of a booley village. Follow the course of the river — through the fence at the flood gate — to meet either of the forest roads on which you go west to the surfaced road at Tomies.

Distance: 8km/5miles. Ascent: 700m/2,300ft. Walking time: 4 hours.

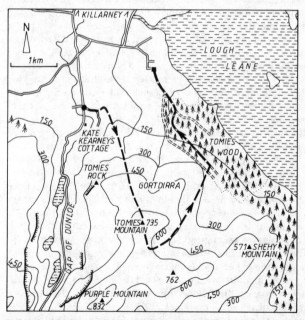

Reference OS Maps: Killarney National Parks or MacGillycuddy's Reeks (1:25,000).

17. (KERRY WAY 2) BLACK VALLEY-GLENCAR

The second day's journey takes us through the lonely and rugged glens of mid-Kerry. One mountain pass, on the Lack Road, is at the 365m/ 1,200ft level and you should be prepared for this.

The first glen is the Black Valley/Cummeenduff (*Com Ui Dhuibh*, Black Corrie) and as you leave the hostel (865 827), you get your first glimpse of its lake-studded floor. The valley rising northwest towards Lough Googh holds some of the remains of an American Douglas Dakota C47 which hit the ridge in December 1943.

Disregard the unsurfaced road rising uphill to the north, marked unsuitable for traffic — this winds its way through the dramatic ice-carved Gap of Dunloe and could be used as an escape route to Killarney. Continue for some time on the road marked cul-de-sac until you reach a Y-junction and go straight on, guided by the first of three Forest Walk fingerposts. Near the junction stood a Mass Rock, used for secret worship in penal times. According to the local legend, the cliffs facing east by the waterfall on your right mark the burialplace of the last Viking invader and it is said that a gold hoard lies with him. As the road rises north, swing left at the fingerpost, zig-zag at the houses in Cloghernoosh (*Clochar Nuis*, Rock of the New Milk) and follow the third fingerpost through a gate. A stony and generally wet path above the stone-walled fields leads directly to the wood. Just before the stile beside the gate, enjoy the view southwest beyond Cummeenduff Lough of the waterfall on the upper Gearhameen River. The path, still stony and wet, winds pleasantly through the wood, which contains enough deciduous trees and holly to mask its commercial intent. Exit by stile and follow the path (keep right) to the grove of pine trees sheltering the next farmhouse. Please close the gate on the far side when through. A short stretch of surfaced road becomes green road again leading into Curraghmore (*Currach Mor*, Big Marsh).

Pass the two houses on the lower (left) side, follow the path (above stone-walled fields and below the wire fence) and continue west to cross the river from Curraghmore Lake by the footbridge. Now on the Bridle (Bridia?) Path, Ireland's highest peak Carrauntuohill (*Corran Tuathail*, Inverted Sickle), 1,039m/3,414ft, lies directly north. The dangers of the ground are obvious and no one should venture to higher levels unless experienced and fully equipped. The cardinal sin is to travel on one's own. As you rise up the path marked by stone cairns, watch for the first of a line of hay markers leading right on the approach to the crest of the saddle. The standing stone on the summit is one of an alignment but while it might seem to be a marker for travellers, it would deceitfully lead you through rough grounds and into the fields of the Bridia Valley ahead. The name (*Na Braighde*, the Prisoners) probably arises from the enclosing rock faces. One of the rocks on the saddle has an obvious cluster of St Patrick's cabbage, *saxifraga spathularis*, another of the rare Lusitanian flora.

Its spatula leaves and pink flower point to its relationship with the domesticated London pride. Once again, please resist the temptation to pick.

Keeping right with the marked path, the descent through rock benches lends relative justification to the name of the townland on which the next house sits — Cappeenthlarig (*Ceapaigh an Chlaraigh*, Plot of Level Ground). Passing through the farmyard should remind you that you are passing, by courtesy of farmers, through their work- and living-place. Please respect all crops, close gates carefully, avoid provocation of working dogs and in case somebody is resting, be as quiet as you can. 2.5km/ 1.5miles from the house leave the surfaced road at Maghanlawaun (*Macha an Leamhain*, Milkingplace of the Elms), the entrance right to the Lack Road being beside a water spout. Despite its name, the trees most seen are the orange-berried rowan/mountain ash and the fuchsia with its red bells. I spent some of my school holidays here. One memory is of being able 'to see the weather approach'. The orientation of the valley is such that rainclouds borne by the prevailing south-westerlies could be seen at its far end long before reaching here and if one was engaged in haymaking, by hand of course, there was time to take action.

The surfaced road here is an escape route to Glencar or to accommodation, particularly if mist keeps you off the pass ahead. The Lack Road (*leac*, flagstone) was used within living memory for droving cattle to the fairs in Killorglin to the north, a journey starting at midnight to ensure arrival at the fair at 7.30 a.m. Before that, the road was used to transport firkins of butter to market by packhorse. While it is much clearer later on, the road has been absorbed into fields initially and you must follow the markers and stiles to gain open hillside where the Lack Road intelligently switchbacks to save energy. As you ascend, you have a view southwest of coombe-enclosed Cloon Lake. An island on the lake is reputed to be the burialplace of William Francis Butler who tells in his book *Red Cloud* of his childhood in Glencar and his later life in America where he joined a Red Indian tribe. Cloon also has an Early Christian site.

At the stile at the summit of the pass, the view northeast is of the 975m/3,200ft Caher (*Cathair*, Stone Fort — perhaps of the Fianna). Beneath you to the north is the amphitheatre of Derrynafeana (*Doire na Feinne*, Oakwood of the Fianna) and Lough Acoose (*Loch an Chuais*, Lake of the Recess). With a view further north to Killorglin and Dingle Bay, the vista lends credence to tales of day-long deer hunts by the Fianna, Ireland's legendary army aided by giant wolfhounds. Keeping left to avoid steeper ground on the right, descend the zig-zag road to join a path which starts where the Cummeenacappul Stream (*Coimin na gCapall*, Small Coombe of the Horses), flowing from the slopes of Caher, joins the Gearhanagour Stream (*Gaortha na nGabhar*, Woodland of the Goats). The path leads to farmhouses, the first of which are owned by the Taylor family, a name we shall meet again.

A link from Derrynafeana to Killorglin town and onto the Dingle Way is proposed. If you are interested, watch out for signposts. Alternatively, this may be your starting point on the Kerry Way.

Just past the second set of buildings, watch for the path left commencing in fields and taking you across bogland west of Lough Beg (*Loch Beag*, Small Lake) and over a stepping stone/rock bridge west of Lough Acoose. As I write, news is coming in of identification by archaeologists of a pre-bog system (walls, huts, enclosures and bog trackway) between the two lakes. Before turning left on the surfaced Killorglin-Glencar road, take time to enjoy the view east into the magnificent corrie of Coomloughra shaped by the ridge connecting Ireland's highest peaks, Beenkeragh, Carrauntuohill and Caher. The road left descends beside the Gortmaloon Wood (*Gort Ma Luan*, Field of the Plain of Lambs), through which tumbles the Caraghbeg River. At the Y-junction, bear left to walk 1.6km/1mile to the Climber's Inn. The hostelry, which is also the Post Office, is run by Sean Walsh, an experienced climber. Nearby is the Glencar Hotel, formerly Lord Landsdowne's shooting lodge. One of its renowned guests was Father John Sullivan and it is said that a religious reading overheard at a french window, still preserved, led to his conversion to Roman Catho-licism. Assuming that you have pre-booked accommodation, Glencar is an ideal place for an overnight stay.

Distance: 20km/12.5miles. Ascent: 480m/1,600ft. Walking time: 6¼ hours.

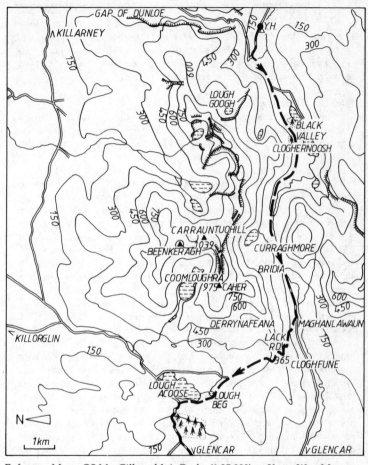

Reference Maps: OS MacGillycuddy's Reeks (1:25,000) or Kerry Way Map Guide (1:50,000).

✓ Did

18. CARRAUNTUOHILL

Carrauntuohill (Corran Tuathail, Inverted Sickle or Serrated Peak) is, at 1,039m/3,414ft, Ireland's highest peak and stands as a challenge to any hill walker. *Climbing it is rewarded with a sense of achieving 'the roof of Ireland' and also with views that understandably are vast. But be warned — this is not mere hill walking and there is some severe scrambling. I suggest that you re-read the Introduction regarding precautions and clothing.*

18(a) The Hag's Glen

The usual route has been from the north via the tantalisingly named Hag's Glen (Coomcallee) and Devil's Ladder. For that reason, I give a description even though, given the state of the Ladder, I have some doubts about the route. Other possibilities are outlined below.

Two access roads lead south each side of the Gaddagh River from the road which runs along the north side of the MacGillycuddy's Reeks from Dunloe to Glancuttane/Glencar. The more westerly one runs over a narrow bridge and, with limited parking below the Y-junction, leads directly to the green road which provides easy walking deep into the glen. The easterly one has become the accepted approach. It passes what was Carrauntuohill Youth Hostel (shown as Gortboy School on some maps) and ends in a farmyard at Mealis (836 873) where you can park your car. The house is that of Joe and Eileen Cronin, who are so happy to open their home for regular mountain rescue call-outs. From here, with the peak already in view, a track or line of a pipe can be followed to cross by stepping stones a stream and the Gaddagh River and meet the green road. If the Gaddagh is in flood, be careful — it has caused one death. It is best to remain east of the river to cross south of Lough Callee. Otherwise, having crossed, you can continue along the green road beside which runs the pipe-line (it also marks a newer, better ford) to Lough Callee (*Loch Chaillighe*, Lake of the Hag). Here can be seen the recently constructed inlet for the Mid-Kerry Water Supply which is the reason for the scars along the glen. Hopefully, these will in time become green and less noticeable so as to recreate the bleak virgin valley as a worthy access route to Ireland's highest peak. Kerry County Council are to be complimented on complying with a request from the Irish Geological Survey Office not to tap the nearby Lough Gouragh (*Lough Gabhrach*, Goat-frequented Lake) where the delicately-balanced moraine trapping the water could have been damaged by any work.

Despite the signs of man's hand, the walk in the glen has solidly severed the contact with concrete and asphalt, and by the time you leave the green road to sit between the two lakes, the solitude is almost tangible. On the west side of the glen, the scree slopes of Knockbrinnea merge into the sheer rock walls of Cummeenoughter (*Coimín Uachtar*, Upper Coombe) with tumbling waterfalls. The eastern side of the glen with two lake-filled hanging coombes completes the picture of Ice Age sculpture. The back-drop is truly magnificent — you need go no further to have had a worth-while day's walking.

It is difficult to believe that this glen was once populated — the 1851 Census showed that six persons were living close to the Ladder. A *cailleach* (hag) also lived here from the end of the eighteenth to the middle of the nineteenth century but the word cailleach more properly meant an unkempt woman. Her existence has been confused with the stories in the folklore of many countries of a hag caring for a child, and it is said that there is a rock on the east side of this glen showing the marks of their feet. Stories are also told of the hag attempting to jump the glen while chasing her lover and falling into one of the lakes. This may be an allegorical explana-tion for floods (caused by rock-falls into one of the lakes or by flash thunderstorms) which from time to time raced down the Gaddagh River to sweep away bridges and houses in their path. One such flood occurred in 1916 and you may have noticed the signs on the high banks of the Gaddagh below your parking spot.

There are more reliable records of another resident in the form of poems in the Irish language. These were composed by *Sean An Gotha Bhinn* (Sean of the Sweet Voice). Sean Cron O'Sullivan was a native of nearby Ballyledder and was a herdsman for the Mealis townland which stretched in as far as the Devil's Ladder. It is obvious that, despite his lowly role in so lonely a spot, or maybe because of it, he was a learned man. His brother, *Seamus (Cron)na nAmhran* (Seamus of the Songs) was also a poet who herded in Coomasaharn — another deep peaceful coombe southwest of Glenbeigh.

The Hag's Glen shows many moods. When the sun shines, this is a pleasant place to rest and reflect. But when the mist swirls and the wind rises, the other face of the Reeks can be seen. It is worth recording here that most mountain accidents in the Irish Republic have occurred in this area. This should be borne in mind as you contemplate moving on.

The Devil's Ladder (the name was surely invented by, or for, Victorian travellers) is the scar running to the saddle southwest of the two lakes. The map shows a path leading as far as the saddle but if it ever existed, it is not now to be seen. However, keeping Carrauntuohill on your right, you are funnelled into the Ladder. Sheep tracks run first to the left of a stream and later, as the ground rises, to the right until you surmount a large outcrop. From here, the going is rougher. Depending on the recent weather, the clay underfoot may be either extremely loose or just loose. This, coupled with a rock field that is easily disturbed, creates the need for utmost care in what is a very steep ascent (150m/500ft in 200m/220yds). Large parties should remain close together rather than scattered along the Ladder. In that way, a rock which tumbles will not have gathered speed before hitting anyone. In the past I have suggested ascending by the left-hand wall of the Ladder where traces of sheep tracks may be found.

However, traffic and erosion wreak such changes that a different course must be plotted on each visit.

From the boggy saddle, there are views now down into Cummeenduff (Black Valley) and the Bridia Valley as well as views much farther afield. From here, the scree-covered slope of Carrauntuohill rises up to the northwest. Follow the cairned route to the peak (or if there is perfect visibility, you can keep a more westerly line to give a less steep approach to the ridge coming in from Caher). The cross on the top is in view from the time you leave the Ladder and reaching it gives a great sense of achievement.

The cross and a windmill to power bulbs were erected here in the summer of 1977 by the people of the Parish of Tuogh as an everlasting symbol of the light of their faith. The cross replaced a timber one erected in 1950 (Holy Year) which lasted sixteen years or so. Some who go into the mountains to seek relief from modern technology may feel that there is no improving on God's work and that leaving nature as he created it would do him greater honour. Nevertheless, this is the form of devotion which seemed fit to those in whose parish Ireland's highest mountain stands.

There is no need to detail what can be seen from the summit — the canvas is vast. I have a hazy recollection — it is 35 years ago — of being able to look north and follow the coast of Clare until it faded at Galway Bay. Such days are rare of course and you will have to satisfy yourself with what is given. The peak's closeness to the Atlantic in the path of the moist south-westerlies means that it seldom lacks a cloud cover.

An eye to the weather should be kept at all times — do not let the views cause you to tarry. To avoid the cliffs on the descent it is even more important than it was on your way up to follow the cairns which, given the amount of rock, do not always stand out as you might wish. Many people have taken the wrong route off the top with sorry results. On the Ladder, caution is again required — many find the steep descent more trying than the climb. If nervous, throw your pride to the wind and descend on your backside! Once the saddle between the lakes is reached it is 'plain sailing' home.

Distance: 11km/7miles. Ascent: 920m/3,000ft. Walking time: 5–6 hours.

18(b) Alternatives

Many climbers now use Cummeenoughter as an access but this is only for the experienced. The coombes are steep — three climbers were badly injured by an avalanche some years ago — and the final leg is by way of the precipitous Beenkeragh ridge. Two other possibilities can be considered. From Breanlee, you could climb via Caher and return also on that route (Walk 19). Particularly if coming from Kenmare or Sneem via Ballaghbeama, you could ascend from the Bridia Valley using the Lack

Road to gain the ridge to Curraghmore (Walk 17) and onto the second summit of Caher (Walk 19), starting either from Cloghfune (766 812) or Maghanlawaun (777 816). Time and distance are not quoted. Perhaps you should not be off the conventional route if unable to prepare a route card.

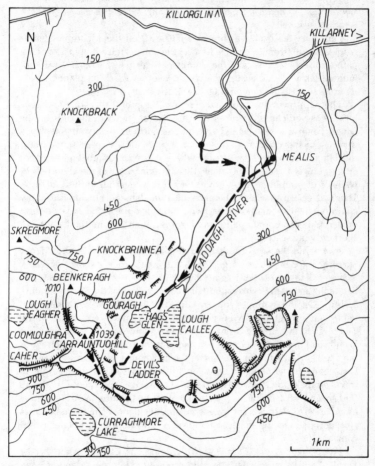

Reference OS Map: MacGillycuddy's Reeks (1:25,000).

19. COOMLOUGHRA HORSESHOE

Including Ireland's three highest summits, the circuit of Coomloughra must be regarded as the country's finest horseshoe walk. This narrow ridge gives a far greater sense of being 'on top of the world' than the previous approach to Carrauntuohill. One word of warning: the route is not for those of a nervous disposition.

Park near the bridge at Breanlee (767 867) on the Killorglin-Glencar road. Go south from the bridge to meet the bohereen leading to a winding path on the western side of the Cottoners River which drains the Coomloughra lakes. Please ensure that you do not encroach on planted fields (or cross fences) and that all gates are closed after you.

The path turns south behind a rock outcrop and then east and very quickly as you climb by the side of the stream, views of the hills on the Dingle Peninsula open behind you; they are most impressive if you have a covering of snow, although this may not be the time of year to undertake the Horseshoe. Cross the stream where it leaves Lough Eighter (*Loch Iochtar*, Lower Lake). At this stage, there is a fine view of the almost sheer walls of the amphitheatre. Carrauntuohill rises over all to the southeast. The hydroelectric scheme here resulted in damage not envisaged by environmentalists and planners who did not oppose the idea of clean power. One can only hope for rapid revegetation despite the height and short growing season.

Ascend northeast to the sharp summit ahead — this is the shoulder of Skregmore (*Screag Mhor*, Large Rough Hill) and there is a short ridge walk to the peak (848m/2,790ft). From this point, there is a further rise and fall before the ascent to Beenkeragh (*Beann Caorach*, Peak of the Sheep: 1,010m/3,314ft). On the summit, you are already 'above it all' with hills and valleys all around and a view across the plain of mid-Kerry to the north. The ridge to the cairn of Beenkeragh (one upright stone in the centre) has been broad and rocky. Now it becomes almost a knife-edge, a place perhaps to be avoided if rain has made the lichenous rock slippery. It seems best not to travel along the top but to descend slightly to the right to travel on the Coomloughra (west) side at this stage. You should be able to find sheep tracks. Barren as the area seems at first glance, there are flora in abundance. St Patrick's cabbage is much in evidence. The ridge becomes steeper as you swing north to the peak of Carrauntuohill to take a welcome respite.

From the peak (1,039m/3,414ft), leaving the cairned route to the Devil's Ladder on your left, descend carefully to join the ridge to Caher. You travel west-southwest on sheep tracks to the left of the sheer drop into Coomloughra. There are three summits to Caher, the second (990m/3,250ft) being the highest. From the second there is a ridge (left) to Curraghmore but keep more right to rise up the steep scree slope to the third peak (975m/3,200ft). From there, you can continue northwest to pass over a spur (442m/1,581ft). My preference is to get out of the boulder field as soon as possible by descending carefully before reaching the spur to the eastern end of Lough Eighter and joining the track by which you ascended. The road made beside the pipeline is usable but very steep.

Distance: 12.5km/7.75miles. Ascent: 1,150m/3,750ft. Walking time: 6/7 hours.

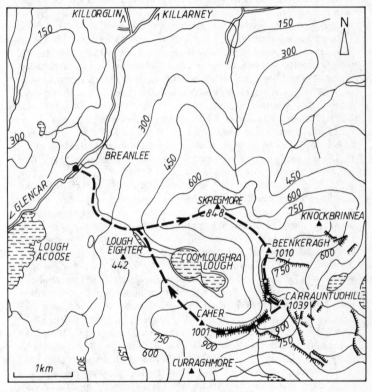

Reference OS Map: MacGillycuddy's Reeks (1:25,000).

With no less than six peaks over the magical 915m/3,000ft, this is claimed to be the finest ridge walk in the land. An organised walk was, at one time, held each year on the June Bank Holiday, stewarded by the mountaineers of Kerry. However, logistic and environmental considerations led to its abandonment. In any case, it had served its purpose in introducing so many to the Reeks. It is a walk for experienced walkers only and careful calculation must be made of the time required, allowing for the composition of your party.

Park your car opposite Kate Kearney's Cottage (881 887). From there, walk up the road into the Gap of Dunloe for about 0.5km/0.3miles. A green road on the right zig-zags towards the summit of Strickeen Hill (440m/1,446ft). This is a welcome bonus on the first leg of the journey. The road (a turf bog road, in fact) ascends as far as the scarecrow trees on the skyline — you can omit the 440m/1,446ft summit — and then swings south to take you into bogs and in line for the first peak, *Cnoc an Bhraca* (731m/2,398ft). The slope is rich in hurt (whortle-berry). This peak is the turning-back stage for some who now realise that they were over ambitious. If you have cause to return, **do not attempt to descend to the beckoning road below to the east in the Gap of Dunloe** — this course has led to more than one accident.

Having savoured the view south to Kenmare Bay (origin of the Ice Age floe which shaped the Gap of Dunloe), head west-southwest down to the saddle over lake-dotted Alohart. From there, climbing begins and the steep and sharp scree-covered slope is a good hint of what is to come. On one journey here, a colleague (Father Aengus Fagan of Rochestown College) photographed a circular rainbow broken only at the bottom by his own shadow. This is how a rainbow should appear but those of us who do not fly much and are generally earth-bound do not see rainbows in full. I have a colour slide of Father Aengus photographing the rainbow but why I did not shoot the comparatively rare optical phenomenon itself I could never explain afterwards. The slope ends at the 932m/3,062ft *Cruach Mhor* (Large Stack) which is surmounted by a grotto. An old man living in Ballyledder below is responsible for this — he had to haul everything, even the water, in plastic bags to the top for his act of worship.

The 'interesting' part of the walk now begins. There are two arêtes — knife-edges — lasting for approximately 1.5km/1mile. **If your head is not good, do not press on!** The passage can be made easier by dropping down on the first leg to meet a sheep track on the western side, bypassing the 939m (unnamed) peak in the centre and crossing the ridge top to continue to second leg on its southerly side to arrive at the peak 988m/3,191ft, generally known as Knocknapeasta. This peak is named after the lake-corrie below, Coomeenapeasta (*Coimín na Peiste*, Coombe of the Serpent). If the sun catches it, you may see the wing of an American plane which crashed into the lake during World War II. On a course for Cornwall from

North Africa, it was flying too far west. Seeing the Dingle Peninsula, the crew believed that they had overshot their destination and flew south into the Hag's Glen, realising this too late to gain sufficient height to clear the ridge. Further wreckage was found on the Cummeenduff side in an area where rare plants were being catalogued. Continue now west-southwest over points 973m and 926m (*Bearna Rua*, Red Gap) to the 958m/3,141ft *Cnoc an Chuilinn* (Hill of the Rolling Incline). From there, the ridge continues west over *Cnoc na Toinne* (846m/2,776ft). There is a wire fence just before this summit and this is a sign that you are well into the second half of the walk.

From *Cnoc na Toinne*, descend to the boggy saddle over the Devil's Ladder and up the scree slope to Carrauntoohill. Incidentally, there is a well — which unfortunately dries up in the hottest weather — on the cairned line to the summit. From Carrauntoohill, follow the line of the previous walk over Caher down to Breanlee.

Distance: 18km/11miles. Ascent: 1,830m/6,000ft. Walking time: 7½–9 hours (it has taken 12 hours or longer!).

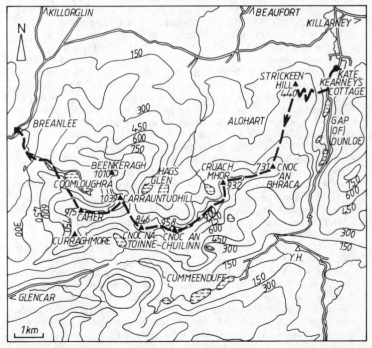

Reference OS Map: MacGillycuddy's Reeks (1:25,000).

21. MULLAGHANATTIN

Mullaghanattin (Mullach an Aitinn, Summit of the Gorse) is a 773m/
2,539ft peak southwest of the Reeks, high point of two horseshoe walks,
one from the Glencar side and the other from the Sneem side.

21(a) The Cloon Horseshoe
This offers great variety but you must be prepared to regard it as an all-day walk.

The usual starting-point has been from the summit of Ballaghbeama Pass (754 781) from where there is an interesting scramble to the top of Knockavulloge (462m/1,505ft) and from there an ascent of over a mile to Mullaghanattin itself. Incidentally, if you have reason to return on this course, instead of heading north to the Pass top at Knockavulloge, a more easterly course is essential to avoid the steeper ground.

A start at Ballaghbeama, while it means that you can complete the entire horseshoe, also means arranging for two cars, one of which can be left at Lettergarriv. If only one car is available to you, I suggest parking it on the main Cloon valley road near the Owenroe River (725 801), walking up to the houses at Cloghera and seeking permission to walk through the fields (use and close all gates). Mullaghanattin (773m/2,539ft) from this side looks perfectly conical and you walk up the spine between the two gullies, one containing Eskabehy Lough. On my first trip here, I had just been initiated into the joys of plant-life. This sharp slope (involving some scrambling, particularly nearing the summit) is rich in some of the rarer plants which I could recognise — sundew, butterwort, St Patrick's cabbage, to mention a few. I was surprised to see a solitary woodbine apparently growing out of a rock. Given the outline of the mountain from this side, it is surprising on arrival at the summit to find a broad boggy top bare of stone — a few stones have been found to pile on one another as an excuse for a cairn. Views aplenty are given — across the plain north to Caragh Lake and Killorglin, east to Lough Brin (there are stories of a Lough Ness type monster in that lake) and southeast to the Kenmare River/Bay.

As you descend west-southwest to the next saddle, look south across the Pocket. The rocks laid millions of years ago are exposed to view and so rippled that one could imagine them still pliable and moving. Just above this saddle is a tablet commemorating the death here in April 1973 of Dublinman, Noel Lynch. Noel was an international climber killed in a simple fall while hillwalking.

The next leg of the journey, south over Beoun (752m/2,468ft) and then southwest, is generally a pleasant stroll along a grassy ridge with views south across coombe and plain to the sea. If you have tarried earlier and the day is well advanced, do not let smug self-satisfaction overcome you. There is rougher ground ahead. By the time you reach the narrow ridge before Finnararagh, the nature of the terrain to come is clear. Short rock faces and constant ups and downs seem to add enormously to the journey. Of course, if you are lucky in the day and there is good visibility, there is adequate compensation. I cannot claim ever to have had views here. You can bypass Finnararagh and swing northwest on a bearing to take you to the seven lakes trapped on the rock shelves over the sheer walls at the back of the coombe above Lough Reagh. I repeat sheer walls — **no attempt should be made to find a descent at this point**. If you are in need of an escape route, there is a steep gully leading down from the flat slabs north of Coomalougha Lake. However, on past experience, the descent is so slow and the route across rough ground west of Lough Reagh and, worse, the bog between it and Cloon Lough equally as slow, that nothing is gained. It is as well to continue on the horseshoe.

From the lakes, ascend to the unnamed summit of 666m/2,185ft. Before heading north, make sure that you are on the summit — a broad boggy expanse — well above the rock faces over Lough Reagh. From the top, the line of the shoulder is quite clear and it takes you to the houses at Lettergarriv, some distance from which you will have been forced to park your car. If in the mood for further exploration, you could detour into the bog just south of Cloon Lake to visit an Early Christian site with interesting stone carvings, marked Cillin/burial ground on the map.

There are roads on both sides of Cloon Lake to take you to your parking spot.

Distance: 14.5km/9miles plus road walk. Ascent: 1,040m/3,400ft. Walking time: 6/7 hours plus time on road.

21(b) Around the Pocket

A shorter circuit, perhaps for shorter days, is provided on a southerly approach. From the R568 (Sneem-Killarney road), take the Ballaghbeama Pass road and turn southwest through Tooreenahone to the end of that road where a house stands sheltered in bushes (745 755).

A rough unsurfaced road leads across a stream and into the coombe — it is clearly shown on the map — from which a direct assault on Mullagha-nattin can be made. However, the rise is sharp and I think it best to travel from the house east-northeast to point 534m/1,754ft from where the circuit can be done anti-clockwise. Care is, of course, necessary in the descent at end of day.

Distance: 9km/5.5miles. Ascent: 820m/2,700ft. Walking time: 4½ hours.

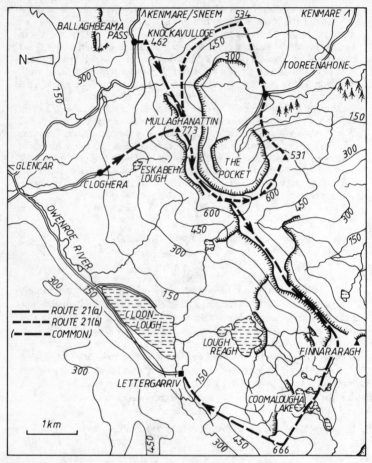

Reference OS Maps: (a) Sheet 78 (1:50,000); (b) MacGillycuddy's Reeks (1:25,000).

22. (KERRY WAY 3) GLENCAR-GLENBEIGH

The third day's walking is through the valley of Glencar (Gleann Chartaigh, Rough Glen, possibly Glen of the McCarthys) following the course of the Caragh River, ending at the seaside resort of Glenbeigh.

Opposite the Climbers Inn/Glencar Post Office is a pleasant green road leading southwest between rock outcrops. As you emerge onto a short stretch of surfaced road, you are looking directly at a mountain pass, Ballaghisheen (*Bealach Oisin*, Pass of Oisin). Oisin was a Fianna warrior lured by a fair maiden to *Tir na nOg*, the Land of Youth. Having spent a number of lifetimes there, he pined for his former companions and was allowed to return to Ireland on condition that he did not dismount from his steed. He stooped from his horse to help weaker mortals then living in Ireland to move a large stone. Unfortunately, he fell and instantly advanced to his true age. He spent his last few years recounting the deeds of the Fianna to Early Christian monks.

Cross the Upper Caragh River at Bealalaw Bridge (*Beal an Labhaid*, Mouth of the Watercourse). An inspection of the waters beneath reveals its clarity. The river is so unspoiled by artificial fertilisers and other contaminants that it was used to establish a baseline for judging the purity of European waters. The river has provided good fishing for generations and, when in spate, there is excellent whitewater canoeing. Through a gate on the far side of the bridge, follow the riverside path used by anglers. Some of the pools are deep and care should be taken not to go too close to the crumbling bank. Across a footbridge, turn left to follow by a stream over footbridges courtesy of Coillte Teo. and right onto the forest road. This leads firstly through commercial planting and later older wood-land of birch, holly and oak. As you pass Drombrane Lake on the right, look east for another view of Coomloughra Horseshoe. Just after the lake, you join a surfaced road for a few hundred metres/yards before entering left through the next forest gate. A well defined path winds gently uphill west and north to a viewing rock commanding Caragh Lake. The path winds down to emerge on surfaced road near Lickeen House.

If time permits, turn right along the public road to Blackstones Bridge beyond the picnic area. Having enjoyed the view here, a few steps more, east of the bridge, takes you to the site of the Blackstones Ironworks and Welsh village. In the 1660s, Sir William Petty imported tradesmen for his smelter here, using the supply of local wood until it ran out. Welsh surnames — Jones, Taylor, Morris — survive in Glencar as a reminder.

Returning again to Lickeen House, follow the Way uphill on the surfaced road through pleasant woods. Quirkes Shop on the right beyond the House may be a welcome sight if you are in need of refreshment. At the top of the hill, the road swings right. Immediately, between the school sign and Bunglash(a) School itself, take the byroad left uphill until surfaced road runs out approaching the saddle, *Bearna Gaoithe*/Windy Gap. Pause here to look southeast in the direction from which you came. Your entire journey (days 2 and 3) has been through landscape carved in the

Ice Age. Ice moved through Ballaghbeama Pass which can be seen in the distance, through Glencar Valley, scoured out the glen now housing Caragh Lake and then moved north to Dingle Bay.

At this point, you have the choice of two routes to Glenbeigh. You can take the shorter route north through the gate left, over the Windy Gap and along pleasant lanes down to the village. Alternatively, you can follow with me on the green road which travels northeast hugging Seefin above Caragh Lake. This longer route gives magnificent views of Caragh and north over Dingle Bay to the Slieve Mish Mountains and it would be a pity not to take it. True to the placename Bunglash(a) (*Bun Glaishe*, Base of the Streams), a number of rivulets run under the green road, welcome on a hot day. As you travel north, in line with Reen promontory across the main lake, Cappanalea Outdoor Education Centre nestles over the brow. As the road swings northwest, you enter artists' country. Pauline Bewick, her paintings obviously influenced by the surroundings, lives in a cottage below the road. At the saddle at Treanmanagh, join surfaced road. Pause again for the views. That northwest shows the final run of the Caragh River entering Rossbehy creek. The pillars standing in the river once supported a railway bridge and if you stay with us on Day 4 of the Kerry Way, we shall meet further traces of the Great Southern & Western Railway's course to Cahirciveen.

As you continue downhill northwest, the length of Dingle Bay comes into view with the sandy finger of Rossbehy Strand complementing the promontories of Cromane and Inch. Swing left on the N70/T66 to the village. Glenbeigh and Rossbehy (*beithe*, birch) have appealed to families for generations. The Glenbeigh Hotel, said to be the oldest in Ireland, and the Towers Hotel enjoy international reputations and a tradition of accommodating families means that there is also a choice of guesthouse and house to let.

Distance: 17km/10.5miles (the alternative route through Windy Gap is 4km/2.5miles shorter). Ascent: 350m/1,150ft. Walking time: 5½ hours.

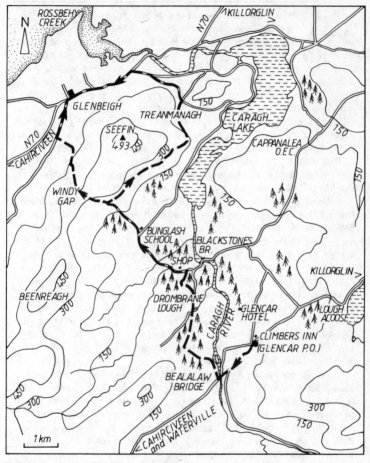

Reference Maps: OS Sheet 78 (1:50,000) or Kerry Way Map Guide
(1:50,000).

23. COOMASAHARN LAKE HORSESHOE

Our next walk is southwest of Glenbeigh village where the Ice Ages have created a dramatic series of six coombes in an area of approximately ten square kilometres/six square miles. It needs a fine day because it would be a pity to miss the magnificent views and because coombes mean cliffs! I should mention the need to show all courtesies including parking with consideration. As a result of the experience of Coomloughra, the Federation of Mountaineering Clubs of Ireland opposed a hydroelectric scheme planned for this area. Some locals did not agree with the stance taken.

From Glenbeigh, follow the signposts off the N70/T66 to Coomasaharn Lake. Near the lake, the road turns sharply right where a small grove of pine trees surrounds a red-roofed building. Park car here (635 853).

The name Coomasaharn is puzzling. For years, some thought that the name referred to *Satharn* (Saturday), when people might have gathered at the Mass Rock deep in the coombe during the Penal Days. It is now accepted that it originated in ancient Irish and the meaning is not certain. Indeed, this area shows signs of the earliest human presence. There is rock art in the field to the right of the surfaced road going right uphill. Your route to the mountain is straight ahead on unsurfaced road to the eastern side of the lake where you will find a gate. This leads to a fairly steep ascent. Zig-zag through rock benches to the 561m/1,835ft top of Knocknaman (*Cnoc na mBan*, Hill of Women). This follows the principle of ascending the steeper ground and descending more gradual ground. Apart from the question of safety, gaining views (for example, that of the main lake and its serrated shore) more quickly is encouraging and on this walk, there are two extra bonuses: travelling clockwise gives a better vantage over Dingle Bay later in the day and the prevailing wind will probably be with you at that stage.

From Knocknaman, a gradual rise leads to Meenteog (715m/2,350ft) known locally, simply and aptly, as *Muing* (flat, boggy, long-grassed place). If you have kept close to the cliff tops, there is no better place to lunch than over the hanging valley of Coomacullen (*Cum a'Chuilinn*, Coombe of the Rolling Incline). This is a haunt for ravens who may entertain as they dive and soar with the air currents. As you sit, there is a spot visible across Coomasaharn Lake with the intriguing name of Tooreentoninairde (literally sheep pasture, backside up). In the inner end of the main coombe is a rock where local tradition has it that the last wolf in Ireland was killed (by Mayo bounty hunters who apparently travelled the country for the £5 reward given for each head). Incidentally, if your meal has provoked a lethargy, do not feel tempted to descend here. There is no recommended escape route into Coomacullen.

You are now at the southernmost point. Swing west (or slightly north of west) to follow a very definite feature — a boundary wall of an earlier era consisting in places of a stone wall and in places of a straight cutting

(3m/10ft wide or so), presumably where scraws were dug to make an earthen wall now weathered away. This leads to the 772m/2,541ft peak, on the OS map given the unlikely name of Coomacarrea. The high ground here is known to locals as *Sagart* (the Irish word for priest, presumably some connection with the Mass Rock below). The landscape is almost lunar due to the erosion of the turf in places, down to the gravel bed below. From the first top, you descend to a saddle beside a line of stakes, which ends with a line of standing stones. Keeping northwest, ascend through the turf banks up to the rise east of the 760m/2,500ft point (Teermoyle Mountain on the map).

Now, swing north. The spur coming from the right is in view. The 513m/1,682ft peak is called Coomreagh on the map but is called Conaire (*Cun Aire*?) locally. This is gained by a short arête (a knife-edge but not too frightening), to reach which you must descend a grassy slope. The coombes here come so close that you must see where you are going. If mist has caught you, I can only suggest taking a bearing for Gleesk to the northwest. The arête, called *Ceimaconaire*, gives a magnificent view of the L-shaped amphitheatre with the Mass Rock directly across the coombe by the streams.

After the arête, there is a flat boggy triangle. Head for the left peak, with views as you travel of the MacGillycuddy's Reeks. Over Conaire and keep left on the line of the spur to the outer end of the lake (taking care across wire fences or, better still, finding the gates) to gain the road.

Distance: 9.5km/6miles. Ascent: 790m/2,600ft. Walking time: 4½ hours.

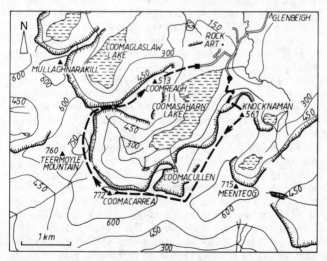

Reference OS Maps: Sheet 78 (1:50,000) or Sheet 20 (1:126,720).

24. (KERRY WAY 4) GLENBEIGH-CAHIRCIVEEN

↑

Glenbeigh is an ideal centre for walking, being close to the higher peaks and having a number of circular low-level routes. You will have gathered already from the last stage of the Kerry Way (Walk 22) that the alternative routes from Bunglasha to Glenbeigh (the Windy Gap or Treanmanagh) provide a circuit. In describing the Way ahead, I give three routes from Glenbeigh to Coolnaharrigle, allowing you to select one if travelling on or combine two if remaining in the area.

Leave the village (67 91) on the western end, departing from the N70/ T66 immediately, to take the road for Rossbeigh beach, crossing the narrow stone bridge over the Behy river. Turn right and walk to the picnic/parking area on the left.

Start (a)

From the picnic tables, join the forest path, and follow it at it swings back, walking approximately 600m/650yds. When on the left you can see through a gap in the trees that you are in a straight line with Glenbeigh's single street, look for a path winding uphill through the trees. This is narrow and barely visible but already beginning to be well-trodden. At the upper end of the wood, go over the fence and continue up the heather slope to meet, coming up from the left, a stone fence surmounted by wire sheep fence. Go close to it as soon as possible to avail of the well-worn sheep track. Your views right are of Rossbeigh strand and left of the Windy Gap and its green road on which you may have travelled yesterday. At the top of the first summit, over the fence is an unpretentious heap of stones, presumably a prehistoric burial mound and known as Laghtshee (*Leacht*, Monument; *Si*, Fairy?). As you rise, the eye is drawn inevitably across Dingle to Inch spit and the Brandon area. Already, directly behind you, you will have seen the ruins of a castle, Headley Towers, generally called Winn's Folly. This was built for the fourth Baron Headley who was responsible for the infamous Glenbeigh evictions which received much publicity in the London *Times* and were the subject of debate in the House of Commons. As you reach the summit (275m/905ft) of Curra Hill, to the southwest can be seen the three coombes of Coomasaharn — many of the evictions took place in that area. Ironically, looking north, you can see one of the improvements made by an earlier Lord Headley — the rampart across the back strand of Rossbeigh which once enclosed 500 acres on which crops were grown.

Descending to the saddle, disregard the double track of tractor wheels coming from the left on the far side of the fence and continue on the right of the fence up the next rise to cross a stile at the fence corner. Descend leftish then to meet the new road ahead. This was recently cut to the western summit where hang- and para-gliders can benefit from sea breezes for take-off. As you gain the road, in the middle distance you can see the Early Christian route ascending above the fields on Drung Hill and, beginning in a grove of trees, the Middle Ages road on which the Kerry Way continues. Coming off the para-road, walk past the pleasantly-named house, *Ard na mBlathanna* (Height of the Flowers) to the surfaced road where you go left and down, noting the old stone fence covered in vegetation on the left, to a cross-roads. Go right here and downhill, disregarding any lefts or rights until you come to another crossroads. Here, the surfaced road goes left and you should follow over a bridge across the N70. In the townland of Coolnaharrigle, you are now at Mountain Stage Railway Station — the N70 is built on what was the railway line until the Farranfore/Cahirciveen spur was taken up in 1960. The name, Mountain Stage, comes from an earlier form of transport, stagecoaches — after the ascent from Glenbeigh, horses were changed here. Crossing the bridge, you come to a T-junction with the old road. If in need of refreshment, there is a shop a short distance on the left, the last one between here and Cahirciveen. The Way continues right past two white stonefronted bungalows on the left. In the garden of one is an example of prehistoric rock art.

Start (b)

As I write, there are some technical problems in completing the marking and erection of stiles along the route of the first start. If you are in doubt or if a good Irish breakfast leaves you unfit for an early morning ascent, you can remain on the forest path and contour through wood around the south side of the hill. This leads to a stretch of surfaced road, quiet and bordered with hedgerow of fuchsia and blackberry briar. You arrive at the first crossroads below the para-road, where you continue straight and go left at the next crossroads to reach the bridge at Mountain Stage.

Start (c)

The third option takes you along by Rossbeigh beach. For somebody doing the route in reverse, the idea of an evening swim on a beach manned in summer by lifeguards may appeal. Pass the picnic area and continue on the surfaced road to the beach. On the left are a number of attractive stone houses shown on the map as Retreat Lodges. These were built for British Army officers when an artillery practice range functioned, 1889–1898, on the beach. Continue past the Ross Inn uphill a short distance and take the right fork at the Y to follow the road over the sea. Well within living memory, there were fields and houses between the road and the sea but erosion has swept all away. As you reach the first cluster of houses on the left, you may see evidence of a landslip which caused the total destruction of a bungalow just a few years ago, the result of an underground spring rather than the sea on this occasion. Just past the two-storey house on the left (with a seat perched on the cliff edge across the road for full enjoyment of summer sunsets), you come to the end of surfaced road and can see up on the left beyond the stream the outline of a green road ascending to the saddle to the south. Straight ahead is a farmhouse, with haybarn on the left. Go right and left behind the house and seek out the green road. As I write, bushes crowd the entrance but these vanish immediately to offer gentle climbing on a road that took motor vehicles up to 20 years ago. Earlier, those who tilled the fields used this road to carry on their backs baskets of seaweed for use as fertiliser. Over the summit, cross the stream at the small bridge, join surfaced road, go right at the crossroads and then left to meet the bridge across the N70.

Reverse Route

Because of the multiplicity of roads here, I feel it best to give a brief description for those travelling the Way in reverse — west to east. Coming off the green coaching road, go right and then left to cross the bridge over the N70. Now right at the crossroads before deciding on one of the three options. If you want that swim at Rossbeigh, take the next left to the small bridge and green road and then right to the beach. If not, continue to the next crossroads and either straight on to contour to Glenbeigh or left and right to meet the para-road and take the ridge top over Curra Hill and the forest path.

Returning to the east-west route to Cahirciveen, all options converge at the bridge and share the right turn to the rock art. A short distance after, watch for the start of a green road in a grove of trees on the left. The start is narrow, so wet that the carniverous plant butterwort can be seen. However, it soon opens out. This is often called the Coaching Road and is known locally also as the Butter Road, a reminder of days when firkins of butter were taken by horsemen to the Cork Butter Exchange which provisioned the ships of Europe. As you travel westwards, you pass a number of heaps of stones, perhaps the remains of houses. One house was well known to eighteenth- and nineteenth-century travellers and it stood at Kilkeehagh near the rudimentary bridge. The house was called *Bothan na nUbh* (Hut of the Eggs) where an old woman sold eggs to those passing along the road. It is believed that the egg store was probably a front for a shebeen. After the bridge, simply follow the stiles to contour on the clearer green road giving spectacular views over Dingle Bay. A look at an OS map shows the line of the road from Cahirciveen (over Foilmore Bridge to Boulderagh — the right angle near Limateerha) to this point from where it descended to Coolnaharrigle to continue north of the Behy River to Glenbeigh Village and run in a straight line as far as Killorglin. The road builders of the period were known to favour straight lines whatever the terrain and while we follow much of it on the Way, circumstances force detours on occasions. Here, the builders lovingly created a road over a slope which runs straight into the sea (pause to look at the stonework of the banks on each side). One can easily imagine the terror of travellers in swaying horse-drawn coaches. It is recorded that Daniel O'Connell the Liberator was thrown from his carriage when the horse fell along this road on the way to or from Derrynane. Arriving at the saddle under *An Fhiacail* (The Tooth), the pointed peak on the left, you can view the line continuing southwest through Coomshanna (*Cum Seannaig*, Coombe of the Fox) to meet the wood ahead.

A detour (or further circular walk) can be made by swinging south-east around *An Fhiacail* to the upper saddle (380m/1,250ft) where *Leacht Fhionain* (Monument of St Fionan) stands. You are greeted with even better views southwest of the Valentia River Bay at Cahirciveen. The *Leacht* bears a worn ogham inscription and a cross is scratched on the eastern face. It is said to mark Fionan's grave and there was a tradition of rounds here (penitents, shoeless, walked clockwise around the stone while saying prayers). The site and the practice of worship may have been a pagan one christianised by early churchmen, as the name *Leacht an Daimh* (Ox's Monument) is also used. If you wish to return to Glenbeigh, leave the *Leacht*, descend through bogland to meet the field fences below and contour the slope of Drung Hill at the 300m/1,000ft level until you can take a sharp swing left to follow a wire fence northeast down to Coolnaharrigle.

Resuming the main route west again, as you cross the bogland of Coomshanna still on green road, the footbridge and stile leading into the forest are clear, facilities again provided with the co-operation of the staff of Coillte Teo., the Irish Forestry Board. Seen below on the right, Gleensk Viaduct is a reminder of the Great Southern & Western Railway. The route through the forest preserves the line of the old road, with stiles provided to allow entry to and exit over fences. Beside a sheep pen, there is a forest gate right, a further point of escape to or access from the N70. Exit from the wood and keep on straight. Lichen and growth on the stone fence now lining the road confirms its age. Up a slight rise, you descend to a hamlet of abandoned stone houses, which are worth inspection. While there are signs of modern usage, features such as the open hearth with storage holes on the sides authenticate the traditional design. Descend to meet a surfaced byroad (escape route to Kells) and walk along it for no more than 250m/yds until it swings left uphill. Follow the old road which continues below it. There is a short boggy stretch with views right to Kells Bay. At the next saddle, pause for the view of Valencia Harbour — the name is from the Irish *Cuan Bheal Inse* (Harbour of the Mouth of the Inlet) and nothing to do with the regular influx of Spanish fishermen. Across bogland to the southwest, the line of hillocks provides the route of the Kerry Way to Mastergeehy and Waterville — but that is for another day. The straight line to Cahirciveen has become surfaced road and for that reason, we will be taking a bow-shaped detour to the south. For the moment, continue straight over a series of stiles beside gates down to surfaced road at Limateerha.

A church tower shows over the trees and you aim left of this along a quiet stretch of surfaced byroad made more pleasant by a verge dotted with fuchsia, montbretia and in season, blackberry bushes. Emerging from the shade of the wood that lines one side of the road, you can see, up on the right, one of the Stations of the Cross on Knocknadobar, a modern place of pilgrimage unlike the *Leacht* left behind us. At the T-junction, the road leads right to the church. The road straight on would be a shorter route to Cahirciveen town and as a fingerpost indicates, there are guest-houses even nearer.

The Way enters left through a passage at the left gable of the house, through three gates down to the log footbridge especially constructed for you. Once across the river, go diagonally right through the field and follow markers and stile to a second (concrete) footbridge across the River Ferta. Turn right on the surfaced road for approximately 400m/440yds. Just past the football pitch, a laneway left leads uphill (with ample evidence of bovine movements) before the Way turns right via stiles and gates to unsurfaced road. Go left and then right, past the Art Studio and house snuggled into the hillside. The green road rises giving views right of Deelis Generating Station (turf/peat burning) and ahead the old Cahirciveen Workhouse. Before the next gate, you meet at Tearagh the junction of the Kerry Way. Left is the main route onto Mastergeehy. Straight on through the gate is the spur to Cahirciveen and on the assumption that you are following that, the description takes you that way.

Meeting surfaced road, follow it — straight on but rightish at the first Y-junction and straight but leftish at the second at Bahaghs — to cross the Cahirciveen-Ballaghisheen road and enter a bog road. On your right now is the Workhouse glimpsed earlier. This was built like others during the Famines in the 1840s to provide some charity and much work for the starving populace. Through a gate and over a stile, you are now on very tussocky bog — take care not to twist an ankle. Keep right and follow the path on the near bank of a stream, although at one stage stream and path merge forcing you further right. Keep watch for a marker guiding you into the next field right, then keep straight onto the next laneway, through the gate and on to surfaced road. As directed by the fingerpost, go left for 400m/440yds approximately, and then right to cross the log footbridge. Keep left beside the wire fence to gain a green (bog) road. Here you may inspect turf/peat cutting in progress. Once this was labo-riously harvested by hand for household use. Nowadays it is likely to be cut by machine and much of it goes to the local generating plant. A less salubrious feature is the town dump (left). Shortly after that, the road is surfaced. Continue, go right at the T-junction, cross the bridge over another tributary of the Carhan River and keep straight to meet first the old stone bridge and later the new bridge (under construction 1990) taking the N70 across the Carhan. Nearby are the ruins of Carhan House, the birthplace of Daniel O'Connell the Liberator. Go left for Cahirciveen town.

Distance: 28km/17miles. Ascent: 700m/2,300ft. Walking time: 9 hours.

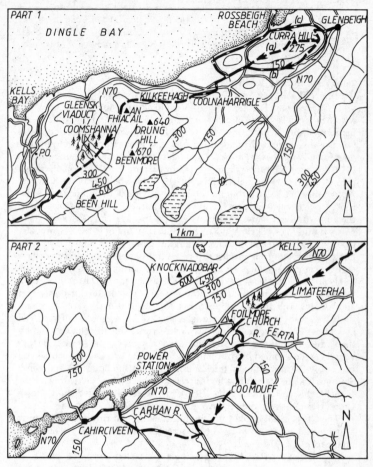

Reference Map: Kerry Way Map Guide (1:50,000).

As one travels on the N70/T66 a few miles east of Cahirciveen, the five-mile-long, scree-covered slope of Knocknadobar (Cnoc na dTobar, Hill of Wells) stands invitingly to the north. It presents a number of easy walks, two of which I describe.

25(a) The Pilgrims' Route

Off the N70, take the road to Coonanna Harbour and at the col before it, you will see a small grotto at the right-hand side of the road. A sign there reads 'Stations — Next Gate'. Enter the gate (482 826) and the route of the Stations of the Cross is quite clear. The faces of the Stations are painted white as are all through gates. At first, the line is more or less northeast but later it zig-zags to ease the ascent and allow time for reflection and prayer.

The fourteen Stations were erected in 1885 by Canon Brosnan, parish priest of Cahirciveen and builder of the O'Connell Memorial Church. Apparently, his second church, sitting under the hill in Foilmore, was de-roofed by severe winds each winter for a number of years. One winter, the roof survived and the Stations were a thanksgiving. Whether there was a tradition of pilgrimage here before then, I do not know. At any rate, there is a Holy Well (at the back of James O'Donoghue's house, the neatly hedged one before the grotto) dedicated to St Fursey and said to offer a cure for sight complaints. This was the original start of the pilgrimage route but is not used nowadays as it involves crossing fences. The Stations route is generally wet underfoot, a condition which should favour butterwort and sundew. The first is in evidence but, for some reason, not so the second.

If you want to avoid the moisture, you could begin at the Holy Well (ask James O'Donoghue for permission to cross his fences) and ascend by the spine — an interesting scramble over sharp rock, the sharper part of which can be avoided by dropping slightly to the left. On this course you meet only the eleventh and (after a broad barren shoulder) the fourteenth Stations. Either way, following an ascent which gives increasing views with height, you arrive at the High Cross, generally called the Canon's Cross. Here, Mass is said on the pilgrimage revived in recent years.

The Cross is not at the true summit. Continue northwest straight over a turf expanse, eroded to reveal the scree beneath. There is a small cairn on the 690m/2,267ft peak.

If you have not decided to retrace your steps, proceed east to a shoulder and down to an arête over Glendalough Lakes nestling in the coombe to the north. Needless to say, care must be taken on this short stretch of narrow ridge which leads down to a fairly broad saddle, known locally as the *Mullach* (Top). Here, the path called *Cnoc na mBo* (Hill of Cows), used for driving cattle from Kells to Cahirciveen Fair, crosses the saddle. Attractive as it may seem, abandon any idea of going north on the path into the coombe to follow the route above the sea to Coonanna. This is very rough going and requires a number of detours to avoid deep gullies running down to the sea. Instead, swing right (southwest) to follow the path downhill to meet the line of an old road. This is the *Bothar Ard* (High

Road) which ran from Roads (the townland) to Kells Lake to Coonanna. The road is not always fully discernible and in a few places is somewhat overgrown. The line is generally shown by the ruins of stone dwellings. Approaching the Holy Well, the road becomes clearer and even fitted with a stile or two — I imagine it may have been a short cut to the former school-house to the west (more recently a residence of ex-President O'Dalaigh). If you lose the path, you have only to go south through fields to the surfaced road which will lead you back to your car.

Distance: 10km/6.25miles. Ascent: 400m/1,300ft. Walking time: 3½ hours.

25(b) From Roads

The second walk would be an ideal one for somebody holidaying in Kells. Roads is the townland to the west of the bay with an intriguing name, *Na Roda*, thought to mean an anchoring place for boats. From here, follow the left-hand road at the Y-junction to join the path of *Cnoc na mBo* (526 871). Along the path as it travels into the coombe are a series of stone walls. These are called *Clochans* and were used to support ricks of turf cut nearby for firing by the forty families who lived in this townland in the early part of the last century. The path gives a very gradual ascent to the saddle from which you make your visit to the Canon's Cross.

Your descent can be over the east peak (636m/2,087ft), from which you should travel east and east-northeast to follow the shoulder and avoid the steep descents near Roads Lough.

Distance: 9.5km/6miles. Ascent: 700m/2,300ft. Walking time: 4 hours.

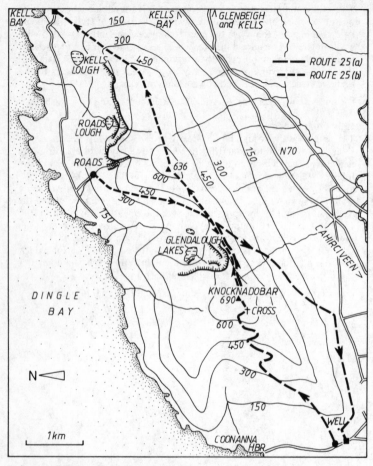

Reference OS Map: Sheet 20 (1:126,720).

26. (KERRY WAY 5) CAHIRCIVEEN-WATERVILLE

This leg of the Kerry Way travels inland along ridges but still giving views of seascape.

Leaving Cahirciveen on the N70/T66 (towards Glenbeigh), stay on the western/right-hand side of the Carhan River. In other words, do not cross the new bridge (if constructed) or the old stone one serving the N70. Retrace your steps of yesterday (see Walk 24 for full description) by — in brief — crossing the bridge over the tributary, going left on surfaced road which becomes bog road, over the log footbridge, left for 400m/440yds, right through gate, onto laneway, keep right at fields to meet the bank of stream, left across tussocky bog, out on short bog road, across the Cahirciveen-Ballaghisheen road, and finally straight to go through the gate at Tearagh. Here you meet the junction where you can bear south (right) to Coomduff.

As you walk over a series of stiles on the right side of the wire fence which roughly follows the double-hump-backed Coomduff ridge top, below you on the right are the ruins of Killinane medieval parish church. It features a fine doorway. In the graveyard are hundreds of unmarked Famine graves, perhaps a connection with the Workhouse nearby. The church is shown on the map and known locally as Srugreana Abbey and the pleasant name (*Sruth Greine*, Stream of the Sun) evokes a picture of monks happily tending bees and making intoxicating mead. Watch for the herd of wild goats which roam here.

As you approach surfaced road at a saddle, Coars National School is below you on the left. Cross the stile onto the road and over a second stile onto mountain. Using the series of stiles, keep left of the main wire fence, over Keelnagore Hill (258m/845ft). Climb to the 376m/1,235ft summit Knockavohaun (*Cnoc an Bhothain*, Hill of the Cattleherd) which mercifully is the highest point reached today — but worth it for the view. Below, on left and right, you can see turf-cutting for the generating station. Almost directly east is the pass of Ballaghisheen and the ridge of the MacGilly-cuddy's Reeks. West is the Atlantic with Portmagee joined by bridge to Valencia Island. Behind, there is a glimpse of Dingle Bay and the Slieve Mish Mountains. Descending from Knockavohaun, do not follow the fence as it swings southwest (right) but cross it to carry on straight using twisty Cloonaghlin Lough across the valley as a reference. As the Inny River comes into view in the valley below, travel by the right-hand side of the stone fence with wire top. Watch for a marker sending you right onto a farm road at Canuig.

The surfaced road leads right and left to cross the River Inny at Foildrenagh Bridge and takes you onto the Waterville-Ballaghisheen road at Mastergeehy. Turn right to pass the (disused) National School and left up past the post office to the Church. This is an interesting simple nineteenth-century building, unfortunately to be replaced with a modern building some distance away. Go right and then left over a stile beside a gate. You are now on *Bothar an Aifrinn* (Mass Path) and to the left is *Glaishe na mBan*, the Women's Stream, where feet were bathed and shoes put on before entering the church. Pass the farmhouse on the right onto open ground with reassuring markers, then onto a clearer path, covered with scrub and grass. Swing right on a newly-cut farm road section. Back on green road, now barely perceptible but the raised edge gives confirmation, watch for the switchback to the saddle above. Once again, you are at a turning point. The main line of the Way continues south downhill to Dromod (there is registered accommodation at Oughtiv to the southeast) and on to Caherdaniel. Assuming that you are bound there, we turn southwest on the ridgetop spur to Waterville.

The route is well endowed with stiles, thanks to the work of the locals and counting them off as you cross may help with directions. While there is no definite path (yet), stay on the south (left) side of the fence. After the third stile, bear left to the next one.

At the lowest point of the ridge, the pass before Knag at Caherbarnagh, the ruins of Dromod church are below on the right, sacked by Round-heads as we learn on the next stage of the Kerry Way. Just off the ridge-top on the right, there is an Early Christian site and burial ground with a slab decorated with a cross. To the south is St Finian's holy well. This whole area has a multitude of ecclesiastical sites, the most famous being that on Church Island in Lough Currane below. Incidentally, the range of buildings across the valley to the left is that of a mink farm.

At this stage, you could take the escape route provided by the obvious path leading southwest (left) to gain surfaced road earlier and speed you on to Waterville. Alternatively, after stile number six, watch for the arrow guiding you up to the elongated summit of Knag (272m/892ft). The tenth stile leads to open mountain with markers reassuring you. All along, there have been glimpses of the River Inny, Ballinskelligs Bay and Lough Currane. Now, there is a panoramic view and you may consider it worth your while to sit and enjoy it. The sixteenth stile is a more elementary one (single step) and once over that, you should go diagonally left downhill to the opposite corner of the field to meet a ladder stile leading to a farm road. Stile number 18 at the right of a gate leads to surfaced road. Turn right, pass the multi-coloured house and continue stright on at the Y-junction. Over the fence on the right is a bivallate (two earthen walls) ringfort. The road takes you straight to Waterville village, a popular seaside resort with a number of gourmet restaurants.

Distance: 30km/19miles. Ascent: 920m/3,000ft. Walking time: 9½ hours.

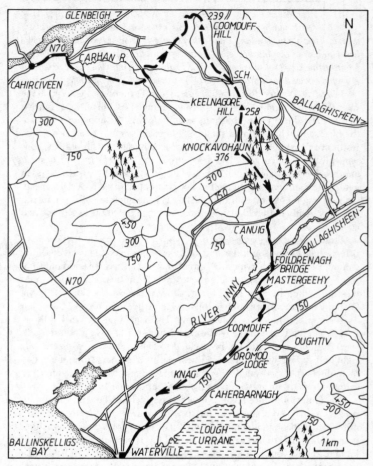

Reference Map: Kerry Way Map Guide (1:50,000).

27. MAUGHERNANE CIRCUIT

The Waterville area has been popular as a holiday centre for generations, particularly for fishermen. It has not always been seen as a walking area, which is a pity. The Inny River valley (between Ballaghisheen and Waterville) has a number of lake-filled coombes on its eastern side. These provide ample scope for attractive horseshoe walks and the one I have termed the Maughernane Circuit is a sample of what is on offer. Walk 29 offers another approach with different views.

Leave the Waterville-Ballaghisheen road at Dromod and go east on the road through Oughtiv to its end at Maughernane (601 698). As you drive in, the view directly into the stony coombe whets the appetite. Opposite the black and white painted (holiday?) house, there are two gates which lead onto the shoulder. A wire fence which crosses your route has, conveniently, a wooden gate. The next wire fence travels with you to meet another at right angles and at the meeting-point there is a further wooden gate. After that, continue up the heather-clad slope for the rock slabs ahead. On reaching these, you find that the line is conveniently with you, taking you very gently to the ridge, where you can look out at the axis of the two coombe lakes.

From this boggy expanse, you get your first glimpse of the Kenmare (River) Bay to the southeast and the views are expanded, on reaching summit 645m/2,115ft, to include Beara Peninsula. (There is some confusion about peak names — so I will not use any.) From this point, you can go west following the faint line of a stone fence. Below on your left is the Glanmore valley, an area rich in folklore. In earlier time, a poet/fisherman lived there and normally fished Lough Iskanagahiny, known locally as *Loch na gCapall* (Lake of the Horses), which is said to have a monster (*ollpeist*) in it. On one occasion, he decided to fish in the two lakes on your right and carried his skin-covered boat on his shoulders from one valley to another. The boat was deliberately damaged and he wrote an amusing satire in Irish (it can still be quoted) about the culprits.

The faint stone fence meets a wire fence which can be followed uphill, passing a small stone sheep shelter, to where it swings left at the flat summit which is the high point of this walk. The map shows two triangulation points (674m/2,211ft and 676m/2,218ft) but this is virtually one flat summit. From its centre, you can look across Cloonaghlin Lough and Lough Namona to the outer end of Derriana Lough. Below, Lough Iskanamacteery is normally called *Lough na hEisce* (Lake of the Esk) after the coombe or gully that runs down to it, *Eisc na Machtire* (Steep Path of the Wolf). Half-way down this, a man once lived and the signs of tillage are still to be seen there. The upper lake in the Glen is correctly shown on the map as Lough Nambrackdarrig (*Loch na mBreach Dearg*, Lake of the Red Trout) and the area around it is called *Cum an Aitinn* (Coombe of the Gorse). These old names remind us that our ancestors were by nature what we have to strive to be — environmentalists.

Continue west from the flat top along the ridge, enjoying views over Lough Currane and Ballinskelligs Bay. As the direct route down from 676m/2,218ft is fairly steep and can be slippery when wet, I suggest that you go to the low point of the ridge before swinging northeast to gain the surfaced road again.

Distance: 4km/2.5miles. Ascent: 610m/2,000ft. Walking time: 2½ hours.

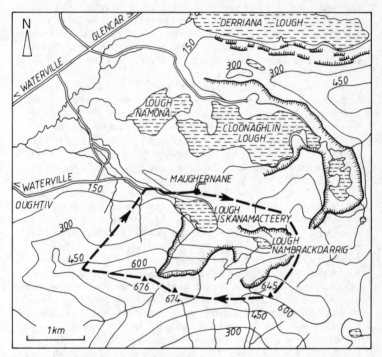

Reference OS Map: Sheet 24 (1:126,720).

Once again, we turn inland travelling from one seaside village to another, immersing ourselves in history on the way. Note that there is a high mountain pass at Bearna Gaoithe *at the 430m/1,400ft level in the second half of the walk, and you should be sure your party is fit both in gear and physique.*

Leave Waterville (50 66), taking the road going east from the grotto to Derriana Lough. The first stage of the way is along the ridge composed of Knag and Coomduff and you can take one of two options left to join it (see Walk 26). You may also continue on the surfaced road to Dromod Lodge which was a hunting lodge. If you are on the main line of the Way from Mastergeehy and descending the southern side of *Bothar an Aifrinn*, on your left is a *gallan*/standing stone.

From Dromod Lodge, cross the road where marked and go diagonally right to skirt the copse of holly, ash, birch and alder down to the Cummeragh River. While there are stepping-stones, it is best to go left through the bottom of the wood to meet the log footbridge especially constructed for you. Across the river, go diagonally left through a field, aiming for the ruined cottage on the skyline. Leave this on your right to follow the line of a cart track which joins a bog road. Ahead is the disused Cahersavane School, its gaping windows giving a skull-like appearance. Leaving the school on your left, turn right on the surfaced road, noting another *gallan* in bog on the right. Behind the first farmhouse on the left is the *cathair*/stone fort of Cahersavane which has a number of *clochans*/stone huts. This fortified farmstead is a miniature version of the more famous Staigue Fort. Go through the gateway left leading to the second farmhouse on the left. It is not necessary to pass through the gateway nearer the house but go left through the small stonewalled fields on a path that looks more like a stream in wet weather. What was again a Mass Path rises right along the slope under cliffs to round the nose of *Mullach Lice* (Head of Flagstones), giving fine views of Lough Currane and Ballinskelligs Bay to the west. Swing left at the summit to descend behind the houses in the almost deserted townland of Cloghvoola (*Cloch Bhuaile*, Stony Milking Place). The stones proved useful on at least one occasion. To the left is *Garrai Chatha* (Gardens of Battle) where Cromwellian troops are said to have suffered one of their few defeats at the hands of the locals who hurled rocks down on them from the high ground above. Descend on the green road through gates to meet the surfaced road and complete the descent into the Glenmore Valley (*Gleann Mor*, Big Glen) through woodland, meeting at one stage an inlet of Lough Currane.

Just before the T-junction, note on the left a holly tree growing from a split rock. If you intended a circuit or are tiring at this stage, the road right is an escape route to Waterville, 7km/4.4miles away. To continue on the Way, turn left here and travel 2.25km/1.4miles to Glenmore School on the right. With falling population, the school is now closed but there has been a strong tradition of education in the area. Before the development of the State system, Glenmore had three 'hedgeschools', outdoor learning places generally devoted to classical subjects taught by itinerant schoolmasters educated secretly on the Continent. The building is now *Teach Bhride* (St Brigid's House), a heritage centre with refreshments available during summer months.

1km/0.6miles beyond this at Tooreenyduneen, watch for the avenue on the right, leading to a house. Moss-covered branches of an oak tree resting on a rock form a bridge over your head. In the old days, hides were tanned in this area. *Bearna Gaoithe*/The Windy Gap is clear ahead. This leg involves climbing and if you are backpacking, you will certainly feel the steep ascent. Take care that you do not go astray if there is mist. Past the house on the right, go over a stile and travel through a delightful series of small stonewalled fields, keeping a small stream 50–100m/yds to your right. Onto open mountain and as you reach wetter ground, look for the rare butterwort underfoot. After crossing the first stream, you meet one of a number of stone folds, this in the shape of an inverted question-mark with a hollow in the wall, thought to have been used for milking goats. Continue directly for the pass.

I have no hesitation in saying that the view here is the most spectacular along the Kerry Way and that's saying something! From here you can see the route taken by Cromwellian troops. They landed at Westcove directly below you to the south, crossed this pass, fought and lost the battle at Cloghvoola and, crossing by Caherbarnagh, went on to sack and stable their horses in Dromod church. A ghost is associated with Bearna Gaoithe following a murder during a faction fight. You may care to visit (St) Crohan's Well on the left, on the far side of the saddle. This was noted for curing eye problems especially if a small fish appeared but in the circumstances, you may not wish to improve your sight!

If you are walking from Caherdaniel and the green road has encouraged you on despite mist and you still intend travelling to Glenmore, take care as the descent is steep. Once you meet it, you can use the stone fence on the left as a handrail — follow and do not cross it. You will pick up the markers as you emerge below cloud.

Travelling south, following the steep ascent you will be pleased to learn that there is 6.5km/4miles of splendid green road to ease your way to Caherdaniel. As I write, fencing is being erected but you should have no problem, using gate or stile. On the right, some way down, is a track leading to old copper mines, last worked in 1900. A cave used as a cell by St Crohan is near the mines. You quickly arrive at a Y-junction of green roads. This has been named Camomile Junction because of the profusion of the plant — used in lawns for its strong scent. Tea is made from the flowers for medicinal purposes.

Go right from the junction. While this section was used, up to the 1930s, by children going to school, the road becomes less clear for some time where wet bog has taken over, but the line, greener than the surrounding bog, should be obvious. Against the cliff and conveniently adjacent to a stream is Kate's Cave where sloping rock, built up with stones and sods, made a home. From this humble dwelling, Kate's son went on to become a schoolmaster a hundred years ago and could boast that he came from a house with only one slate. The road emerges through an avenue of fuchsia bushes into the centre of the neat village of Caherdaniel. A stay overnight will allow you to visit Derrynane House, home of Daniel O'Connell the Liberator.

Distance: 28km/17miles. Ascent: 1,000m/3,300ft. Walking time: 10 hours.

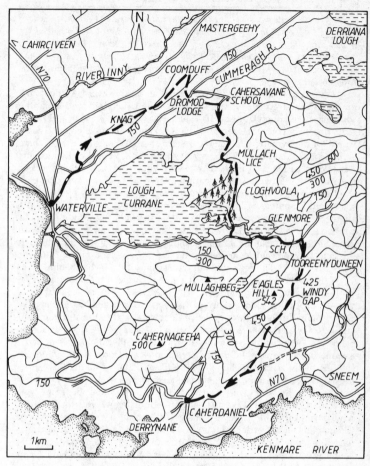

Reference Map: Kerry Way Map Guide (1:50,000).

29. CLOGHVOOLA CIRCUIT

A gentle day's walking using part of the Kerry Way allows an eastern approach to high ground already covered in Walk 27. A disadvantage is that the walk is at the join of two of the ½ inch OS maps, sheets 20 and 24. You may find it more convenient to rely on the sketch map in this book but I recommend carrying with you the OS sheets for recognition and enjoyment of the panorama provided.

Leave Waterville village (50 66) travelling south towards Caherdaniel on the N70 and go left to pass the Waterville Lake Hotel and along the south shore of Lough Currane. If you have to walk, the narrow and twisty road provides constant change of views. 7km/4.4miles along the road, watch for the byroad left along the eastern shore of Lough Currane. There should be a Walking Man fingerpost to show that you have joined the Kerry Way. In any case, the holly tree springing from the split on a rock to the right of the byroad will confirm that you have arrived. Continue through a number of gates on this narrow road, used mostly by fishermen for whom a number of laybys have been provided, until you come to a sharp S-bend. There are a number of farmsteads ahead with regular comings and goings by the owners and only one car can be parked (with consideration) here at the bottom of the S, leaving room for entry through the gate and for vehicles travelling up the S to the next farm. If there is more than one car, it would be better to use one of the laybys behind.

Walk up the S-bend and through a gate onto green road. You have the choice of keeping left on the Kerry Way to *Mullach Lice* (see Walk 28) from where you can take the spine east or you can shorten the journey by aiming now for the highest grove of fir trees straight ahead of you. You cross a track, perhaps the one used by children travelling to Cahersavane School. As you rise, you can inspect the stonewalled field system and I assume this to be *Garrai Catha* where Cromwell's troops suffered defeat. Judging by the name Cloghvoola (*Cloch Bhuaile*, Stony Milking Place), this must have been a booley, a summer pasture where cattle owned by a number of neighbours were sent with a herder. Reaching the spine, you have the Cummeragh River valley spread out before you to the north with beyond it the Inny River valley. To the right are the outer ends of Cloonaghlin and Derriana Loughs. As you rise to the cry of choughs wheeling and hovering over the corrie of Lough Iskanamacteery, the height gives views north to Knocknadobar and Dingle Bay. Behind you are the waters of Lough Currane and Ballinskelligs Bay.

Approaching point 676m/2,218ft, a heap of stones seems to indicate a burial mound — but perhaps it is only a fallen sheep shelter. The extended summit has a triangulation upright on the eastern end. The outer end of Lough Iskanamacteery came into view on the left below before you reached the summit and from the next saddle east, you can peer down into the dramatic coombe. If you have had enough walking, you now have the option of setting a course west-southwest directly down to Cloghvoola. Alternatively, you can continue east onto the next summit 674m/2,211ft with its weather-beaten bog cover. From here turn right to travel southwest on the ridge, gaining views of the Kenmare River and the Beara Peninsula. *Bearna Gaoithe*/The Windy Gap is south of you and directly ahead as you travel on the ridgetop is Lough Coomrooanig nestling high in the hills between Eagle Hill and Mullaghbeg. Look left at the cliff-faces of Tooreens — the layering process is revealed with the sedimentary lines now upright. I seem to remember being told by the O'Connells of Tooreens that their farm contained 160hectares/400acres of rock, not difficult to believe given the view from here.

Having taken in the views, I would caution against continuing too far southwest on the spur as there is very steep ground with rockfaces ahead. It is best to take a course west (right) and pick a gentle course down the gulley near the stream that runs to the houses in Cloghvoola, and use the green road to walk to your car. Incidentally, the figures given below assume you have a car, and they are for the circuit around Cloghvoola only. You must add time if walking from and to the village.

Distance: 10km/6miles. Ascent: 640m/2,100ft. Walking time: 4 hours.

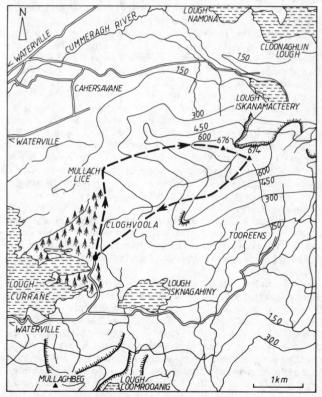

Reference OS Map: Sheet 24 (1:126,720).

This leg of the Way provides walking on the old road between these two settlements in use up to the end of the nineteenth century. The fact that the road is at a higher level than the N70 leads to far better views. Typical of the roads of the period, it is as straight as the terrain permits and it would almost be sufficient to tell you to follow the line. However, a description is given to introduce you to items of historical and other interest.

From the centre of Caherdaniel village (550 594), opposite Freddie's shop, take the narrow fuchsia avenue up past Kate's Cave to Camomile Corner (see Walk 28) where you rejoin the main line of the Way.

Take the lower route straight (east) to meet shortly Kilcrohane (*Cill Crohain*, Church of St Crohan). There is the ruin of a church and two burial grounds, ancient and modern. Rounds were made here (and at the holy well at *Bearna Gaoithe* above) up to the last century between 29 July and 1 August. The dates suggest that the practice descended from the festival of the pagan god Lug.

The surfaced road yields to green. Two small rivers at Behaghane can be crossed by wooden bridges before joining the next section of surfaced road. After 2km/1.25miles or so, as the road swings left for Staigue Fort, the Way continues straight over an ancient stone bridge. The detour is 2km/1.25miles to Staigue which must be looked on as the best example left of a fortified farmstead, with internal steps leading to the ramparts. The construction may be as old as 500 BC.

Back on the main line, a short distance beyond the stone bridge on the right just off the road is an example of prehistoric rock art. There is no sign and if you are interested, you may need local direction. The absence of a sign prevents vandalism. Ascend to the saddle, not forgetting to take in the views behind of the island-dotted coastline. At the summit, there are more views of Kenmare River (Bay). Downhill, on the obvious line of the road, in sight of the more obvious green road to the next saddle ahead, a mini-footbridge leads to a field and you exit through the gate (be sure to close it) to the surfaced road at Bohercogram (could it possibly be *Bothar Chograim*, Road of Gossip?). 75m/yds of surfaced roads leads back to green road. Pause at the stream for a refreshing drink before ascending this pleasant stretch of green road, so well-preserved that one could visualise the horse-drawn coaches of the last century. Here and earlier, the wet ground holds a profusion of plant life prospering in the acid soil but I was surprised to notice under the road by one of the streams hidcote growing wild. Enter Gortdromagh Wood, a firebreak preserving the straight line. Unfortunately, on the far side of the wood, the bog is so wet that the road has been devoured. It is best to take the forest road right before the wood ends to join the N70, staying on this for about 700m/800yds past *Coill na Muine Fluiche* (Wood of Wet Neck) before taking the first surfaced road left. Swing right to the original line past a cottage, immediately onto green road, over another short stretch of surfaced road and once again on green which takes you much of the way to the village of Sneem already in view ahead. The magnificent corrie/coombe of

Coomnahorna is on your left. Less than aptly named Derry West (*doire*, oak-wood) appears just as you see surfaced road ahead, there is wire across the green road — the old stone bridge was destroyed by flood. Look for the gate on the left to a path leading you diagonally down a field to a footbridge. A number of footbridges have been constructed to ease your journey along the Way under the skilled instruction of forester P. J. Bruton. This is probably his most ambitious undertaking and you can doff your cap in tribute to him and the builders as you contemplate the tumbling waters below. Go right and immediately left, once again on line to follow less than 2.5km/1.4miles of surfaced road to the neat, colourful and award-winning village of Sneem.

Distance: 18.5km/11.5miles. Ascent: 490m/1,600ft. Walking time: 6 hours.

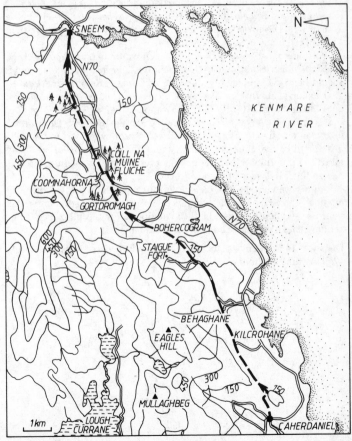

Reference Map: Kerry Way Map Guide (1:50,000).

31. COAD-EAGLES HILL

A day's climb, conveniently using a section of the Kerry Way, is available from Caherdaniel.

At the junction at the centre of the village (550 594) opposite Freddy's shop, enter the fuchsia avenue to follow as instructed in Walks 29 and 30. At Camomile Junction, go left uphill to *Bearna Gaoithe*.

From here, take the short steep rise west up to the top of Eagle Hill (544m/1,786ft). This is locally called Paykeen (*Peicín*, Little Peak). From Eagle Hill, take the ridge slightly south of west to clear Coomrooanig. This is locally said to be *Cumar an Mhanaigh*, Ravine of the Monk. Based on the spelling on the map which would have followed the pronunciation of the last century, I wonder if the monk might not be someone of greater importance and if the name might be *Cum an Romhanaigh*, Coombe of the Roman, a title bestowed on the few who, in the early days of the Christian Church, could make the journey to Rome.

You now must make a choice. You can continue on line to meet the bog road which leads down to Coomnahorna. If visibility is perfect (and it should be to avoid going off course into the steep ground), you could — after making sure that you had cleared Coomrooanig — swing northwest onto Mullaghbeg (511m/1,678ft), known locally as *Beal Da Cab* (Mouth of the Two Snouts). You are now over Inchfarrannagleragh. The *cleireach* (cleric) in question this time was a Parson Watson who lived in the glebe at the end of the nineteenth century and about whom there are many tales. The unfortunate man capped his eventful life by shooting his wife and ending his days in Mountjoy Prison.

All my wanderings here have unfortunately been in bad weather, so I am unable to be too specific about directions. I repeat the admonition that your travels should only be in good conditions. From Mullaghbeg, a line south will take you to the bog road to Coomnahorna.

Distance: 14.5km/9miles, including Mullaghbeg. Ascent: 580m/1,900ft. Walking time: 5¼ hours.

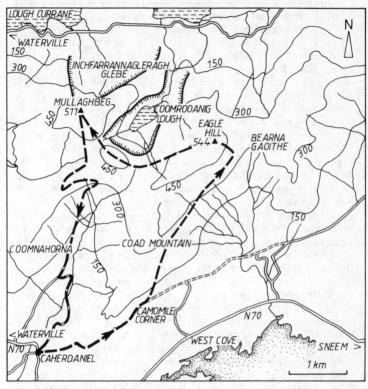

Reference OS Map: Sheet 24 (1:126,720).

109

32. KNOCKNAGANTEE

For those based in Sneem, there is very pleasant climbing to Eagles Lake with its waterfalls and a scramble if continuing over Knocknagantee.

From the western square of Sneem village (66 69), travel north for almost 6km/3.7miles following the course of the Sneem River. Its twisty course gives the village its name (*snaidhm*, knot). Opposite the football pitch, go left at the Y, left at the T (5km/3.15miles) and over a concrete bridge to park with consideration beyond green farm buildings. This is *Glorach* (Noisy), named for the tumbling streams and the echo by the lake.

To the right of the last house (668 712), a farm road winds uphill. You can go cross-country northeast and north, following the tributary of the Sneem River which drains Eagles Lake or you can follow the farm road north, not forgetting to close the gate. As it swings west, leave the road and go onto the mountain through the sheepgate, made of two poles held by wireloop. Again don't omit to secure it — sheep may be confined to higher ground for feeding or, if it is lambing time, confined nearer the houses as protection from foxes. Go uphill through long grass and later barer ground with the waterfalls behind the lake coming into view as you ascend. In wetter weather, the separate falls must combine into one solid sheet. Up on the left are the sheer walls under Knocknagantee. Note the fencing along the top of the cliffs. You should heed the inherent warning — farmers do not want their sheep to wander onto this ground and, unlike you, they have four-leg drive. The stream can be easily crossed at the outlet from the lake, at least in summer. The rocks are lichen-covered and you need to be careful if they are wet. In this hidden corrie, you may wish to linger. Wild duck were to be seen on my visit.

From the lake, care must be taken in picking a course. I stayed on the right of the waterfalls, going up the grass slope and then scrambling/rockclimbing under the dark overhanging rocks near the top of the saddle. Here, in wetter ground, were examples of the carniverous butterwort. Reviewing the course, I feel it would be best to go to the left side of the falls to scramble up the scree slope and boulder field to Lough Coomanassig (*Com an Easaigh*, Corrie of the Waterfall). Keep left above the lake to travel north-northwest avoiding the bull-nose and cliffs west. The stream acts as a handrail to take you onto wide boggy saddle. Unless you go well east to look down from clifftops into the Inny valley, the views here are not great. However, the MacGillycuddy's Reeks show up clearly to the northeast.

From the saddle, swing south to the summit of Knocknagantee, using the fence seen earlier as a second handrail — there's no need to warn you to remain on the right side! Soon the pointed peak (676m/2,220ft) is visible and you can head straight for it. Approaching the cairn, you can see an opening in the wire at the fence corner — open and close it again with care. There is now a 360-degree panorama — much of Iveragh and Beara Peninsulas. This was one of only three triangulation points on the

Iveragh Peninsula for the original Ordnance Survey 1825–1833. Dingle Peninsula must also be in sight but I could not judge, owing to the haze on my visit. According to local lore, the name *Cnoc na gCainnte* (Hill of Conversations) arose from the practice of meeting here from various townlands while out checking on sheep. A few generations ago, families were large and 'some had to go out' to make room.

A stile leads west over a fence from the cairn and obviously this is the prudent course — on no account should you aim south. You can either continue west to meet the farm road approaching the saddle or pick a course southwest to join the road at a lower level. Either way, the road eases the way home.

Distance: 8km/5miles. Ascent: 580m/1,900ft. Walking time: 3½ hours.

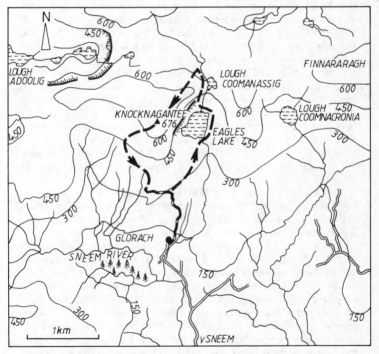

Reference OS Map: Sheet 78 (1:50,000).

As I write (1990), the exact course of the latter stages of this leg of the Kerry Way is to be fixed. However, the earlier stage can be described fully and you will be able to follow markers as you approach Kenmare using the information given here. In general, the walk, like that from Caherdaniel to Sneem, is parallel to and above the N70/T66, once again giving better views, but there is one stretch by the shoreline through Dromore Wood.

Leave the eastern square of Sneem (66 69) on green road starting to the left of the chemist's shop. This travels southeast over a short stretch of surfaced road and further green road to pass an art studio on the right and Askive Cottage on the left on an isolated length of surfaced road not connected to the N70. The forest road through Derryquin Wood follows the course of the old road but, as access through the grounds of Clashnacree House ahead is denied, temporarily at least, watch for the path left which takes you to cross the N70 to the east of the House. West of the House are the Great Southern Parknasilla Hotel and golf course and the site of Derryquin Castle. The hotel grounds are famous for sub-tropical plants and as you travel, you will find that all of the area benefits from the Gulf Stream.

Opposite the electric gates barring entry to Clashnacree, go left on green road to follow the old road again. Local tradition is that this was the route travelled on horseback by Daniel O'Connell the Liberator as he raced to the Cork Courthouse to save a life. Crossing two surfaced roads at right angles, continue east, passing Old Tahilla, a village in ruin. The view right is of Coongar (*An Cuan Gearr*, Narrow Harbour). A stile leads out onto the N70 at Tahilla Church. Just beyond it on the right is the post office and shop.

Continue by crossing the N70 to the byroad opposite the post office. Immediately, go over the fence on the right to resume the line of the eighteenth/nineteenth-century highway. The line is clear, being banked higher than its surroundings, and a line of telegraph poles acts as a handrail. A stile leads into a wood which, as I passed last, looked as if it had been the victim of a whirlwind with isolated groups of trees knocked down. The green road is surfaced shortly after the wood and you travel on this for 0.8km/0.5miles before meeting a T-junction close to where the OS map shows 'Cascade'. You have the choice here of continuing straight on (keep left at the Y-junction) and maintaining the line, but as I write, there are problems at the exit near Blackwater Bridge.

It appears that the Way will go left at the T (watch for markers or follow this course anyway) to go uphill to Derreennamacken to follow an even older road. Considerately, the owner has provided a slip stile to the right of the road gate. 200m/yds beyond, a track follows the spine above the outline of field fences. These were the Tobacco Gardens where cabbage and other produce was grown for sale to provide money for Christmas smoking. The raised line of the road is just visible through the bog and as

I walked it in mid-summer 1990, there was a lush crop of wild flowers with heather just about to bloom. Over the summit (with fine views over Kenmare Bay), cross a wire fence where the raised bank of the road has been devoured by the bog for a short distance. Join the cattle/sheep track. This may have been a route to the former school near Blackwater Bridge and as you descend, markers may send you right in that direction. If in doubt, I suggest you bear left of the abandoned house, part of the roof of which is visible in the grove of trees in line ahead. You can cross a fence to gain the byroad which joins the N70 from the north.

The N70 is a busy but narrow tourist road in summer and you should take care as you cross Blackwater Bridge or peer over at the deep gorge below. Continuing on the N70 towards Kenmare, enter the first gate on the right and follow the forest road. It is worthwhile, leaving this, to go down to the right on the path marked to the Cliff Walk along the shore of Kenmare River/Bay. Across can be seen the glen enclosing Cloonee Loughs and Glaninchiquin. The path winds up left to rejoin the road where you turn right. The road is now fuchsia-lined, a sure sign that there were houses along it. At the Y, keep right beside the high stone yard wall. There is a profusion of montbretia and if it is late summer, there will be a splash of orange flower. The high wall protects the grounds of the Castle of Dromore, subject of the song of the same name. It was once the seat of the O'Mahonys, now in private hands. As you see another high wall in the distance, watch for the marker sending you right to connect with another forest road where you turn left. You are now approaching the N70 but can delay going onto it by keeping right at the Y-junction and joining it after passing the ruins of Cappanacush Castle which stand on the right. Built by the Normans in the early 1200s, it later came into the hands of the O'Sullivans, the last occupant being Col John O'Sullivan, adviser to the Young Pretender and blamed by some for the defeat at Culloden in 1745.

Go right on the N70 continuing for 2.5km/1.5miles. On the right, beside the road leading to the sea at Coss Strand, stands the ruin of a church and a welcome sight on the left of the road is Pat Spillane's public house. Dromoughty Coombe across the bay comes into view as you pass Grenane post office (right) and Templenoe church (left).

At the crossroads, with a signpost for Templenoe Pier, it is approximately 6.5km/4miles to Kenmare town and if it is late, you may consider staying on the N70. Read the description below before deciding. The Way continues on the byroad left, uphill, past the former Ruscossane National School, now converted to domestic use. Once again, the precise line of the Way is to be determined and you must watch for markers. It seems that you must continue beyond the bridge, through two half-circles past Bay View Farm, before finding on the right, as the road straightens out, a track, at present much overgrown. This leads down to the stream crossed earlier. Climb the bank, rich in oak, holly and underlair, to go on to Lacka mountain (*leaca*, flagstones) and travel northeast. Across the fence, you enter a plantation and if a path has not been broken, the going underfoot is rough, wet and full of holes — be careful of your ankles. As I write, the wood plantation has suffered fire damage and this makes it more difficult. In fact, I was so blackened by the charcoal remaining that, having scaled with difficulty the four-strand barbed-wire fence, I treated myself to a hip bath, all that was possible in the stream beyond. Stream it was, during the fine summer of 1990, but I am told that the Reen River can change to a torrent after rain, so a footbridge should have been provided by the time you travel. Cross into a field. A grove of trees inside a fence ahead hides the ruin of an old dwelling. Bear right outside the fence and travel down to meet a track. Exit on to surfaced road over a stile.

Go left approximately 100m/yds on the surfaced road to a stile and Walking Man sign on the right. Follow the series of stiles uphill. Behind, the angle of view has changed again and you now look straight out across the bay. To the right, Kenmare's suspension bridge comes into view. Depending on the light thrown, the two corries of Dromoughty Glen are clearly picked out. Nearer, almost hidden in trees, are the ivy-clad ruins of Dunkerron Castle, an O'Sullivan seat, which gives its name to the Barony. As I write, the final line of markers and stiles is being laid. Even if this does not take you to the summit of Gortamullin Hill (*Gort an Mhuilinn*, Field of the Mill), it is worth making the gradual ascent for the rewarding views towards Moll's Gap to the north before setting a course southeast to follow a laneway on to the N70, where you turn left and then right by the Kenmare Bay Hotel into the town.

Distance: 30km/19miles. Ascent: 520m/1,700ft. Walking time: 8½ hours.

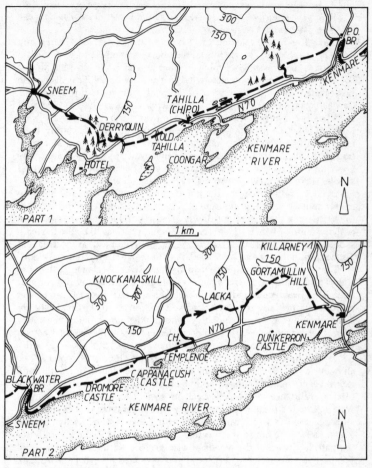

Reference Map: Kerry Way Map Guide (1:50,000).

34. (KERRY WAY 9) KENMARE-KILLARNEY

The last leg of the Kerry Way takes us from the sea via mountain and lake through oakwood back to Killarney.

Leave Kenmare by taking the road past the Holycross Church and primary schools (91 71). At the Y-junction, keep straight to pass the old entrance to the present hospital just before the old Fever Hospital, dating back to Famine times, now converted to a private house. Pass also a fish processing plant and at the crest of the road, your route through *Bearna Gaoithe*, Windy Gap, straight ahead is obvious. Before that, the surfaced road twists down to a little stone bridge over a tributary of the Cleady River. At Gowlane cross, go straight through on to green road. Shortly, there is a stile over sheep fencing and you are now well away from motorised transport which is not to be seen again until you approach Killarney. As you climb, the rock terraces of Peakeen rise on the left. Before the second saddle, there is a new plantation on the left and it is pleasant that the wood is oak rather than the ubiquitous conifer. In the dip, a whitethorn stands solitary watch on the side of the track, a reminder that in former times this tree was never cut down because of its supposed connection with the fairies. There is a gate (heed the request to close it) before the main saddle of the Gap (331m/1,083ft). In view, straight ahead, are Purple and Tomies Mountains across Killarney Upper Lake over Derrycunnihy Wood.

There is now a rapid descent to Ullauns River. A glance at the map shows how many lakes and streams drain into it and at any time of year there is no problem in finding drinking water. In fact, the road can be wet at times, particularly in winter, and you are forced to skirt it. There are some stepping-stones, presumably a relic of olden times. Before the valley floor, there is evidence of a former settlement, the walls of stone houses on the right. Just ahead, a grove of fir trees mixed with oak and rhododendron hides another cluster of buildings, all stone and roofless, one showing signs of recent habitation. As the road loops down through richer vegetation, the cursed rhododendron more obvious now, the only modern residence in the valley can be seen. There is a series of mini-waterfalls to the right of the road and, where streams cross, seek stepping-stones on the left, which can be slippy with lichen if wet. Shortly after the avenue left to the house and meeting surfaced road, keep an eye right for the path leading into the woods at a gorge. The National Park signs tell you that you are at the right place; if you have met the two stone bridges, you have gone too far.

You are now on the leg common to the outward and inward journeys and if you have travelled out from Killarney, you may remember the route. Refer to Walk 13 to remind yourself of the course over Galway's River, through Esknamucky Glen, under Coars Waterfall, south of Torc Mountain and down by Torc Waterfall to reach the N71, travelling on into Killarney by road or via Muckross House and Abbey as you wish.

Distance: 25km/16miles. Ascent: 580m/1,900ft. Walking time: 7¾ hours.

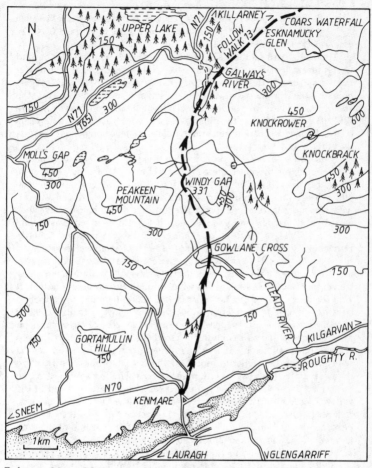

Reference Maps: OS Sheet 78 or Kerry Way Map Guide (1:50,000).

35. DERRYMORE GLEN

Our first walk in the Dingle Peninsula is a pleasant gradual one into the coombe of Derrymore, suitable for a party of mixed abilities. For added enjoyment, the Dingle Geological Guide *should be taken along.*

Travelling west on the R559/T68 from Tralee, 1.2km/0.8miles beyond Derrymore school, is a narrow hump-backed bridge. Disregard the unsurfaced road beside this and take the next (surfaced) road left. Pass one house on the left and park near the Y-junction. A neat bungalow is at the end of the surfaced road on the right. Follow a bohereen which starts here (742 108) and shortly swings right to end at a wire 'gate'. Secure the cable please. Passing a sheep-dipping tank, follow the fence on the left towards the gorge ahead.

Soon you meet what appears to be a dried-up river bed with an embankment across it. In fact, there are ruins of a mill beside the Derrymore River less than 1km/0.5miles downstream and this was the mill race which was dammed each night to gather water. As will be seen later, so were the three lakes inside. From the ruin of a stone house above this, look up at the skyline and you will see what is known to locals as *Carraig a' Tae Pot* (Rock of the Tea Pot, what else?). The old mill race leads to Derrymore River which fed it just below a series of small waterfalls.

Leave the river (the bank is too rough a course) and move right, uphill, to follow a sheep track. There is, in fact, no single defined track but many converging and separating. The ascent through the gorge is gradual. If you are lucky enough to travel on a fine day after rain, the tumbling streams and waterfalls glitter on all sides of this valley, particularly where, after the gorge, the valley opens out to reveal the scree-covered slopes on the right under the cliff columns of Gearhane. Pass a stone wall sheep shelter and continue on a line on the firmer ground at the bottom of the scree, avoiding the wetter ground near the river. Skirting a bowl where the Derrymore River has now diminished to a winding stream, this line leads directly to the first of the three lakes snuggling at the end of the valley. Proceed up the short slope ahead, strewn with massive boulders, to meet the second lake. The southwest corner of this presents an idyllic picture — a small sandy beach under a waterfall with room to pitch a solitary tent. Continue up to the third lake, like the second backed by cliffs.

You might decide to rest on your laurels here but I suggest pressing on. Follow the stream (right) entering the lake from the southwest (sometimes it ripples underground) to enter an amphitheatre where you are in a world of your own. The boulders create many dens. It would be easy to imagine these giving the necessary shelter on a holiday away from it all! Ahead in a clear area below a sheep shelter stands a solitary rock which is, I think, the one known to locals as the King's Table (and presumably also that shown on maps as Finn Mac Cool's Table). The area of course abounds in rocks of all shapes calling for names. What is called the Boat Rock is on the ridge to Gearhane.

Having savoured the isolation, the time has come to return home. The ascent has been so gradual that it may be hard to believe that the inner lake is at the 600m/2,000ft level. This becomes clear when on ascending the rise outside the outer lake, you see — through the gorge by which you entered — the surface of Tralee Bay well below, beckoning you homeward.

Distance: 8km/5miles. Ascent: 640m/2,100ft. Walking time: 3¾ hours.

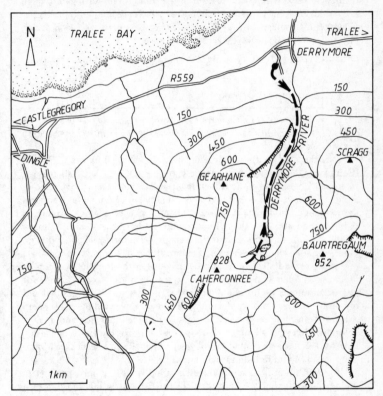

Reference OS Map: Sheet 20 (1:126,720).

36. BAURTREGAUM

The last walk can also be used as an approach to higher things.

From the inner end of the walk, there is an easy ascent travelling southeast (slightly left) to the saddle between Baurtregaum (*Bar Tri gCum*, Top of the Three Coombes) as well as Caherconree which is dealt with separately (Walk 37). From the summit of Baurtregaum, there are the magnificent views of land and sea which are unique to the higher peaks of this peninsula — north across Tralee Bay, northwest to Brandon Bay and south and southwest across Dingle Bay.

Distance: 11.5km/7miles. Ascent: 790m/2,600ft. Walking time: 5 hours.

37. CAHERCONREE

The ascent of Caherconree Mountain is a relatively easy one from the west and this route allows you to take in the prehistoric promontory fort of the same name.

Take the road south, up the Finglas River valley, from the R559/T68 (Camp village) or north from Aughills on the R561/L103 (Castlemaine/ Inch road). This is generally called Bohernagloc (*Bothar na gCloch*, Road of Stones). There is a choice of two starts. Just north of the highest point of the road, at an information/warning board (715 006), a series of markers points out a path. Less than 1km/0.5miles north of that (715 058), maps still show an L-shaped wood at Beheenagh (*beith*, birch). The wood is no more — a few small trees and a greater number of tree stumps remain. I prefer the second start — what must have been the traditional access to the fort also offers better views. Keep to the left of the 'wood', aiming for the rocky outcrop on the shoulder above. The ascent is fairly gradual and my preference for this ascent is because you are rewarded by views on all sides — Tralee Bay on one side, Dingle Bay on the other side and, in fact, before reaching the shoulder, there is also a view of the Lower Killarney Lake to the southeast. Behind (northwest), Stradbally and Beenoskee Mountains shield Mount Brandon from your view.

If you have approached along the spine (look out for openings to underground channels — are they stream beds or is this the line of a fault?), the circular 'wall' with the 'gate' through it and directly in your path looks man-made. This on arrival (600m/2,000ft) proves not to be so but a natural feature adapted by man to his purpose. An almost sheer drop on three sides was complemented with a stone wall on the eastern side to make a promontory fort (a not uncommon feature on sea cliffs along the west coast of Ireland but unusual inland).

The fort (and the mountain) are called after its supposed builder, Cu Roi Mac Daire, a mythical figure with magical powers. It is said that, each nightfall, he caused the fort walls to spin so that no one could enter the gate. He was killed by a ruse worked by his wife, Blathnaid, who alerted her waiting lover, Cuchulainn, that the way was clear by spilling milk which turned the Finglas River below white. The stories of Cu Roi and the other Red Branch figures abound and it may set the mood if you have read them in advance.

From the fort (nowadays referred to by locals as 'The City', a literal translation of *Cathair*), it is worthwhile continuing to the summit of Caherconree (827m/2,713ft) marked by a small cairn. From here, you have a view into the coombe to the north with its three lakes feeding the Derrymore River. The descent can be by the spine or the contouring path.

Distance: 5km/3miles. Ascent: 640m/2,100ft. Walking time: 3 hours.

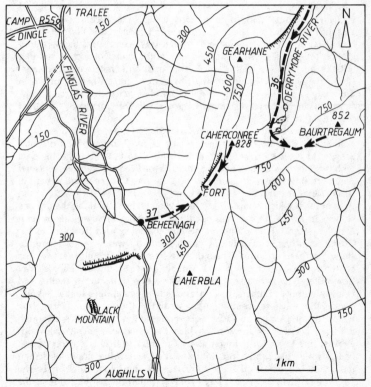

Reference OS Map: Sheet 20 (1:126,720).

38. (DINGLE WAY 1) TRALEE-CAMP

The first day's journey along the Dingle Way (Slí Chorca Dhuibhne, named after the Barony of Corkaguiney through which most of it travels) gives a sample of the views and archaeology for which the peninsula is renowned. The route will be done in reverse on the final day if you are completing the circuit.

In Tralee town (83 14) just off the R559/T68 (Dingle Road) at the Basin, is what remains of a canal built in the 1830s for shipping grain, coal and timber. Where the official signboard stands, the Basin has been filled in, but as you travel west on the path on its northern side, the canal, although silted up, becomes clear and is flooded at high tide. The view of the slopes of the Slieve Mish Mountains to the south gives the flavour of your journey ahead.

Leave the canal path to go left over bridges into Blennerville village. You may detour to the windmill which is still under restoration (1990) and houses tea and craft shops as well as a heritage centre specialising in emigration records. The Way continues west of the village on a track running initially on the right of the R559. This path and that beside the canal earlier make up the line of the narrow-gauge Dingle Railway, of which more later, and you are following it faithfully by crossing the road to the southern side just before Tonevane crossroads with attendant 'Accident Black Spot' sign.

At the crossroads, go left and immediately right, taking a surfaced road uphill past the circular (navy) tank of the Tonevane Group Water Scheme to meet the river. Before the bridge, go right through the gate with the 'No dogs' sign to a picnic table. Please heed the warning, repeated regularly along the Way ahead — you are guests of the landowners in their workplace and this is sheep country. Follow the path west, going right at the Y which is met almost immediately, initially along the top of a stone/earth fence, then across open bogland. Your view right is of Fenit Lighthouse and Tralee Bay, a fine bird-watching area. Just before the Curraheen River, where the bog is particularly wet, a set of stepping-stones has been provided. The old Tralee reservoir is visible below. Cross by the footbridge, the first of a number provided by the Dingle Way Committee. The path rises, passing above one stone sheep shelter and below a number of others, then by another set of stepping-stones — boulders, really — before dropping to the second footbridge over the tumbling waters of the Derryquay River. Set among hollies and birches, although with no evidence of the forest which the placename (*doire*, oakwood) evokes, this is an ideal lunch stop. The next stretch is on top of sod banks/walls, pleasantly soft underfoot and across the slopes of Scragg mountain (*An Screag*, the Precipice) to the third footbridge, over the Derrymore River (*doire mor*, large oakwood). On the western side of the river is a former millrace (see Walk 35). An escape route, if one is required at this time, is provided by the byroad to the R559 below on your right.

Continuing west, we leave the ruggedness of the mountain slopes and the recently-created path behind and, crossing over a stile, descend to come close to the R559 and join (at the right-angle marker) a green road, what must have been the Early Christian route between Tralee and Dingle. For the remainder of today's journey, we follow that line. A second stile leads onto a short stretch of surfaced road past three bungalows. This, another escape/access point, you should note, as the route back to Tralee rejoins here. Back on the green road you meet the crumbling walls of the deserted village and, a little later, the ruins of Killelton church and graveyard (*Cill Eilthin*, Church of Elton, said to be the nephew of St David of Wales). The site consists of a rectangular enclosure containing the remains of a small oratory and two buildings. The construction seems to indicate seventh- or eighth-century building. Restoration work by the Office of Public Works in 1984 led to the discovery of various features and as I write (1990) work is in progress again with a sign warning 'Dangerous building'. By the time you pass, you may find work complete and a descriptive tablet in place. The site has earlier pagan connections as folklore tells that the mound on which the church is built is the grave of Fas.

Continue straight on over a footbridge to meet a very short stretch of surfaced road, returning to green road. The view ahead (northwest) is of Brandon Head and nearer, the Maherees, both visited if you walk the return stages of the Dingle Way. As you crest the hill, your destination, Camp village comes into view. Continue downhill on the green road, across a surfaced byroad (an escape route to the village if darkness is falling) and down again to the Finglas River associated in myth with Caherconree (Walk 37) seen above you to the left. The river is crossed by stepping-stones. A bridge is planned as after heavy rain, short-lived flooding covers the stones — if the bridge is not in place and the river uncrossable, return a few hundred metres/yards and go left for the village. The green road, now narrower between stone walls, rises to the second surfaced road on which you turn right for a gentle evening walk down Glenfais, the glen which I assume gives its name to Camp (*An Com*, the Hollow). As you descend, watch out for two features. 220m/yds from the junction, beyond the first house, to the left of a tubular field gate, you will see a large stone, unpretentious in its recumbent state. This is Faisi's Grave. There is a simple incised cross and an ogham inscription (the letters are strokes above and below a line formed by the upper edge) as well as an inscription in half-uncials. You also will see, on the right below, Curraduff Viaduct. Here, in 1893, the Dingle train speeding east went out of control and crashed over the viaduct killing three crew members and injuring thirteen passengers.

Distance: 17.5km/11miles. Ascent: 275m/900ft. Walking time: 5 hours.

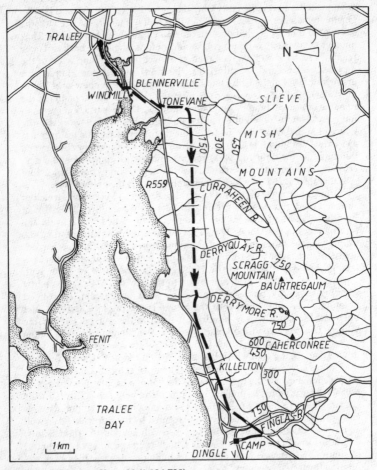

TRALEE

BLENNERVILLE

WINDMILL TONEVANE

SLIEVE

MISH

MOUNTAINS

R559

CURRAHEEN R.

DERRYQUAY R.

SCRAGG MOUNTAIN

BAURTREGAUM

DERRYMORE R.

FENIT

CAHERCONREE

KILLELTON

TRALEE BAY

1 km

INGLAS R.

DINGLE

CAMP

Reference OS Map: Sheet 20 (1:126,720).

The second and later stages of the Dingle Way provide a good deal of walking on surfaced roads. However, most of these are byroads with little traffic and particularly suitable for winter walks if travelling alone.

From Camp village (69 09), travel south on the road starting between the church and Ashe's pub and walk uphill for approximately 1.5km/0.75miles to meet the yellow marker at the junction (end of Walk 38). Just before it on your left is Faisi's Grave. Turn right, again uphill, towards Knockbrack. Initially, the road is enclosed with a high hedge of fuchsia, whitethorn and bramble, blackberry-bearing in autumn. Later, there are views to your left (Caherconree Mountain) and behind (Tralee Bay). However, as we reach the saddle, views west open out. Close to the road going right at the T-junction at Maumnahaltora (*Mam na hAltora*, Mountain Pass of the Altar) is a megalithic tomb with rock art. Members of the Archaeo-logical Survey team were refused entry, so it is hardly worth your while detouring.

The Way continues southwest (left) at the junction and contours west. You are now in the townland of Slieve (*Sliabh*, mountain), country ideal for turf (peat) cutting and sheepgrazing, two pillars of the traditional way of life. Pass a sheep-dipping tank on your right. Aside from providing fuel, the bogs also provided a storage place before refrigeration. There are many tales of findings of centuries-old butter in bogs. In Slieve, a bronze spearhead was discovered, whether in a bog or not I cannot say, but in the next townland downhill through wood, Emlagh (*An tImleach*, the Edge/Boundary), the preservation powers of bog were proven by the discovery in 1950 in land now covered by the wood of a clothed body of a child, thought to be seventeenth-century. Emerging from the wood, straight ahead of you on a hillock is a standing stone inscribed with a Latin cross and now incorporated into a field wall. Locals claim that the place name comes from the fact that it was once the edge of a lake — unlikely, but at any rate, for us the area is a boundary. We again change temporarily from inland to sea views by following the Emlagh River towards Inch where there is a shop and public house.

It is not necessary to follow the surfaced byroad to join the R561/L103 (Castlemaine-Dingle road). Shortly after the Y-junction at Emlagh, watch for the (surfaced deteriorating to green) road on the right, contouring above this seaside resort. Across Dingle Bay, the MacGillycuddy's Reeks are in view. The road changes to a narrow track before you can see the full length of Inch itself (*An Inse*, Watermeadow), a magnificent finger of sandhills some 5km/3miles long stretching into Dingle Bay and matched by two other spits stretching north from the Iveragh Peninsula, Cromane to the left and Rossbeigh to the right. A surfaced road left gives access to this seaside resort. If you are backpacking, the beach may provide camping ground and you may consider a swim. If you are armed with the *Dingle Geological Guide*, the shoreline is one of the localities described in detail and the archaeologist will find traces of shell middens in the sandhills. The Way continues over the short stretch of surfaced road back onto green road uphill at Ardroe (*Ard Rua*, Red Height). Past two dormer holiday homes (note the fibreglass 'thatch' roofs!), go right on the surfaced road and almost immediately left. The surfaced road corkscrews but the green road which we are using maintains a straight line uphill to Maum (once again *Mam*, mountain pass). Tradition is that this was a butter road. In the last century, locally produced butter was taken by packhorse or horse and cart to the Cork Butter Exchange and the journeyman brought back tea and other treats. We are going inland again and you should look behind for a final view. Carrauntuohill, Ireland's highest peak, is centre picture.

Approaching the top, at the T-junction of surfaced roads, continue straight on the road which will take you all the way to Anascaul village. Once over the pass, you are looking straight into Anascaul Glen and Lake. The track winding up the back of the glen may have been the continuation of the butter road to the north of the peninsula. We swing downhill to the village already in view. In a field to the right of the road is the Ballintermon Standing Stone, a prehistoric erection christianised by cross and inscription (now almost invisible due to weathering and use by animals as a scratching post). For those seeking further pre-history, there is a group consisting of a standing stone with Latin cross added, cup-marked stone and possible cist at the foot of Knockafeehane behind the local authority housing estate at the approach to the village.

The village itself is best known as the birthplace of Tom Crean who accompanied Scott on his expeditions. The South Pole Inn is named in his memory. Dan Foley's traditional public house is well known also, the shopfront featuring in many postcards.

Distance: 17km/10.5miles. Ascent: 490m/1,600ft. Walking time: 5½ hours.

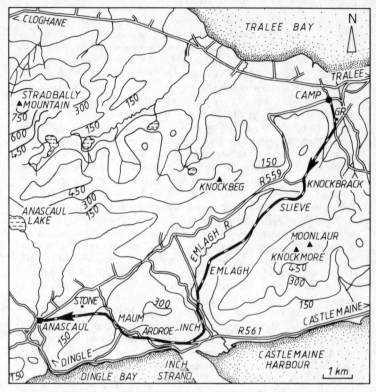

Reference OS Map: Sheet 20 (1:126,720).

40. ANASCAUL GLEN

A further incursion into the legends which are such a part of this peninsula is provided by the circuit of Anascaul Glen.

Travel off the R559/T68 west of Anascaul village on the road signposted to the lake. Park at the car park (584 044). Ascend northwest (south of Carrigblagher Cliffs) to Knockmulanane (595m/1,953ft). The ascent is a long even one with views that become ever more extensive. Underfoot, the grasses make for a surprisingly rich pasture up to a high level. Eventually, you arrive over a gully down which you look directly at the green road beside Lough Anascaul. *Loch an Scail* is named after Scal Ni Mhurnain, one of the many women in whose affairs the legendary Cuchulainn took an interest. It seems that a giant came to take her away and she sought the hero-warrior's assistance. He stood on Dromavalla Mountain, east across the lake, and the giant stood somewhere on this side exchanging fire — boulders no less. After a week of fighting, Cuchulainn was hit and gave a loud groan. Scal, thinking him killed, drowned herself in the lake.

From the cliff edge, travel west to the peak before attempting a descent to the boggy expanse below. Contour to the top of the saddle to join the green road zig-zagging up from the south. This road could, of course, have been used as an access to this point. I have not travelled it but understand from John O'Donnell, who lives in Dromavalla, that the glen is full of interest. Apart from stories of a lake (no longer there) fitted with a sunken round tower and once producing eels 5.5kg/12lbs in weight — as well as a chalk carcass that might have been a turtle's — he tells of Sagart Rock, a V-shaped Mass Rock situated above the sheep-dipping tank a quarter of a mile inside the lake, near which is a well, known as *Tobairin na gComaoineach* (Well of the Communicants). He also tells of splits inside *Faill Dubh* (Black Cliff) 6m/20ft long and said to be 60m/200ft deep. This would be an ideal trans-peninsular walk connected to the Dingle Way. While the green road appears to end at the saddle, maps show the track continuing into Maghanaboe (*Macha na mBo*, Cattle-field) in the Glenahoo River valley to the north. I have heard even of plans to push a surfaced road through to convenience motorised tourists. God forbid!

The green road could also be used to reach Beenoskee (827m/2,713ft) and Stradbally (800m/2,627ft) Mountains, the slopes of which rise to the northeast. However, we are on the trail of Cuchulainn and will continue southeast by the tumbling stream to the cliff edge where we get a spectacular view down the wooded Glanteenassig (*Gleannta an Easaig*, Glens of the Waterfall) and across Tralee Bay to Fenit and Banna Strand. On our first visit here, we were puzzled by a cleared belt which ran along the cliff tops at the 530m/1,750ft level. Rejecting the idea of movement of the earth's surface, we decided that it must be a forest fire-break, obviously a good idea to prevent gorse fires being spread by the prevailing southwesterlies into the new plantations. This opinion was later confirmed by the late Tom Hayes of Killorglin who was the forester-in-charge when this work was done in the 1950s.

The flat top of Dromavalla Mountain (533m/1,750ft), now within easy reach, shows a line of standing stones — locals term them sentries guarding Cuchulainn's House, the large mound of stones which proves to be hollow in the centre. I thought it a natural deposit but archaeologists think it may be a burial mound, the hollow due to the collapse of the underlying chamber. We must leave legend behind and descend the gorse-covered slope to cross the river to the car park.

Distance: 9km/5.75miles. Ascent: 715m/2,350ft. Walking time: 4¼ hours.

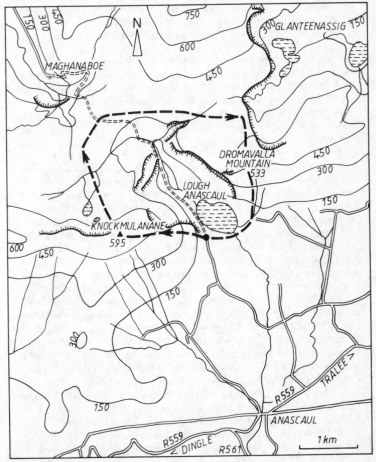

Reference OS Map: Sheet 20 (1:126,720).

Day 3 on the Dingle Way takes you via byroad and remote hillside to the town and harbour of Dingle, now a 'must' for the tourist.

Leave the village (59 01) by travelling west on the R559/T68, and at the Y-junction go left with fingerpost pointing towards Castlemaine (R561/L103). Take the second road right, signposted Minard Castle. The surfaced road rises uphill through the townlands of Gurteen and Acres, contouring above the R559.

As the road approaches Kilmurry Bay and you get the first glimpse of the top of the Minard Castle walls, the road loops down anti-clockwise. At the beginning of the loop, a gate on the left gives access to a flat hilltop on which are the very ruined remains of Cahernanackree (*Cathair na nAcrai*, Stone Fort of Acres). The main reason to visit the site is to admire the view, a feature of all forts. The tutored eye will discern a bivallate (two walls to you and me) fort with the foundations of a rectangular house and a souterrain, in which what may have been a stone mining hammer was discovered in 1940. The bay beneath has a very fine storm beach, the large boulders looking like an artificial creation. The Dingle Geological Guide describes this locality in detail with plenty of illustrations to show how the exposed rock reveals cross-bedding. Minard Castle is thought to be sixteenth-century. There is a sign warning 'unsafe building' — it was blown up by Cromwellian forces in 1650. If you want to risk entering, you will be surprised to find features such as fireplaces and the remains of vaulted ceiling. To the west of the castle are a possible booley, the ruins of Kilmurry Church (*Cill Mhuire*, Mary's Church) and St John the Baptist's Well. If you have time to visit, you can seek directions.

Keep on straight past the beach, in other words left at the Y-junction, and then go right onto a short uphill stretch of green road, changing to semi-surfaced from the cottage on the right and meeting surfaced road at the T-junction. Once again, straight on past Minard School (left) and a colourful house (right), down around an S-bend and then detour left onto a semi-surfaced road giving views of Dingle Bay and Iveragh to the left. A glance behind will show Rossbeigh spit to help confirm how far you have travelled from Inch. Turn right onto surfaced road and continue uphill to pass to the left of Aglish graveyard (*An Eaglais*, the Church) — the mid-seventeenth century church is no longer visible. An ogham stone (lettering unclear) stands beside one of the tombs. At the complex junction, go right and, meeting the original road up from Minard Castle, go left down to Garrynadur. Across the R559 is the Fairy Glen as you can see from the map. The name probably derives from the fact that this area and Gowlane to the west, through which you will be travelling, is full of the remains of forts as well as Bronze Age field systems, all of which must have seemed to our ancestors to be evidence of fairies. You need not join the main road but go left on the quieter byroad which runs on a parallel course to

Lispole village. Once again, we approach the line of the Tralee and Dingle Light Railway and you can see the viaduct over the valley below on your right.

Join the R559 through the village and, having crossed a bridge, turn right immediately. The Way continues straight through the crossroads, 0.4km/0.25miles later. However, if you wish to explore another ecclesiastical site, you should go left there and after 200m/yds or so, enter a gate left. The site is interesting in that *Teampall Martain* (St Martin's Church) is built within a large earthen-banked enclosure which also contains the foundations of three or four houses and a possible souterrain. The church ruin is pre-thirteenth century with later extensions. Returning to the crossroads, you obviously go left and then take the second surfaced road left to travel northwest. Keep right at the Y and watch for the yellow arrow directing you to the right over a stile beside a gate. Carefully close two further gates and go left beside a field boundary to meet green road (with such evidence of animal movement that the value of earlier advice regarding footwear may be proven!).

Passing Devanes' Farm Guesthouse (Lisdargan) on surfaced road, turn right, uphill, for a short distance before swinging left again on another track leading downhill to the fuchsia and fern banks of a river. At present, stepping-stones aid crossing but a footbridge is planned. Go cross-country now, keeping an earthen fence on your left, over a stile and onto another green road, through a gateway and into a farmyard at Ballingarraun. An arrow on the roof-barge of an outbuilding directs through a gate and onto surfaced road. Leave this immediately and go right, up beside a stream, then left (not through the gate) to travel below the field between stone walls. Between you and the sea is evidence of two of the latest cultures — buildings devoted to intensive agriculture (pig fattening) and, nearer the coast, mariculture (fish farm ponds). Two timber stiles of a unique design save you opening and closing gates but the third gate should be closed after you as you reach a farmyard at Ballyrishteen. Join the surfaced road, downhill to a cluster of former habitations, then right and left through a second gateway. Right once more, left through a gate and cross the field to a stile across a stone fence clearly in view ahead. Beyond the fence, railway sleepers form a footbridge allowing you to cross another field to the gate ahead. In view ahead is the Sugarloaf and your line is to the north (right) of it. The view south now is of Trabeg (*Tra Beag*, Small Strand) with its Bull's Head sea-stack appearing from this distance to be a lighthouse. This is another of the Geological Guide localities — you may wish to plan a detour tomorrow. The gate leads to green and surfaced road at Ballybowler.

Leave the surfaced road after 40m/yds or so to go up right, beside a stone fence facing you, and then left on a wide green road. You are now approaching the Garfinny River. Some 0.8km/0.5miles downstream, but not really accessible from here, is a drystone single-arched bridge just wide enough for one carriage, confirming that the route we have been on was the line of the medieval road between Lispole and Dingle. As with the townlands behind, this one shows evidence of habitation going back to pre-history. Two sites of *fulachta fiadh*, rectangles dug into the ground for cooking venison with water brought to boiling point with stones heated in fires, exist on the river bank. To continue on the Way, we go right at the Y to cross a concrete bridge upstream and meet the green road coming down right from the Conair Pass, this undoubtedly being another medieval road in use until the R559 was built in the 1830s/40s mainly to serve coaches but partly to provide relief for those suffering the effects of the Famine. Joining the green road, go left past the two farmhouses at Ballybowler, join surfaced road, cross the R559 and with the harbour in your sights, take a straight line down Ballinasig, past the Hillgrove Hotel and into Dingle town. The attractions of the town are well covered in various guides and an audio-visual show at the heritage centre. I mention only the string of gourmet restaurants, no doubt unconnected with the old saying 'fat as a Dingle boy' but take care that you don't suffer the same fate!

Distance: 19km/12miles. Ascent: 410m/1,350ft. Walking time: 6 hours.

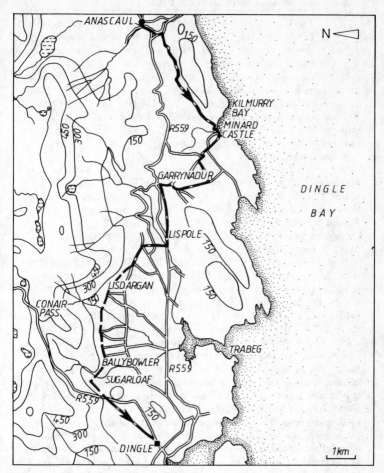

Reference OS Map: Sheet 20 (1:126,720).

42. BALLYMACDOYLE-EASK

This is a short walk giving good views and easily accomplished from Dingle town. Despite a few fences along the course, it would be quite suitable for parties with young members. Wellington boots might be useful in view of the wet condition of the bohereen at the end of the walk.

From the Dingle-Ventry road, turn east and pass the entrance to Burnham, now a girls' college, *Colaiste Ide*. Continue approximately 1.5km/ 1mile on the road until it swings sharp left (424 988). Enter the gate there (the smaller one on the right) and take the path uphill and across fields to the summit of Ballymacdoyle Hill (133m/437ft). An L-shaped shelter provides an opportunity for a rest. Depending on the day, there are even now fine views all round.

Descend to the saddle over the sheer drop into the sea. The bird-populated cliffs are reminiscent of the Skelligs Rock which can be seen out in the Atlantic to the southwest. On a narrow promontory over the cliffs is Ballymacdoyle Fort, known locally as *Leaba na bhFiann* (Bed of the Fianna, Ireland's legendary army).

Ascend now to the top of Eask (189m/619ft). Keep right of the wall ahead across your path — watch the slope — and cross it near the concrete observation post. This was in use during World War II and there is an identical one across Dingle Bay, at Roads near Kells. The tower itself is said to be a warning against a false harbour to the west. This is borne out by the finger on the east side pointing to Dingle Harbour, the entrance of which would not be clear to boats approaching from out in the bay. The harbour and Dingle town now lie below you to the north, backed by the Brandon range of mountains.

Continue east along the ridge top (there are stepping-stones conveniently placed on the first wall that crosses your path). The ridge has now become scree-covered and, by the slope up from the north, one judges that it was smoothed by ice which left the stones in its wake. Directly ahead, between you and Lispole, is what appears to be a lake but a look at the map shows it to be an inlet of the sea from Trabeg.

Reaching the end of the headland, the lighthouse at the harbour entrance with another tower inside it (an old signal station?) can be seen across from you. The mouth of the harbour has been the 'beat' of Fungie, Dingle's dolphin, and you may get a sighting. Keeping directly in line with the lighthouse, you meet the end of the bohereen which leads left to the surfaced road.

Distance: 6km/4miles. Ascent: 150m/500ft. Walking time: 2/3 hours.

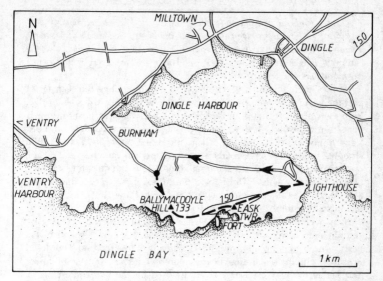

Reference OS Map: Sheet 20 (1:126,720).

While our journey so far along the Dingle Way has introduced us to folklore, archaeology and geology, in my view you are about to sample a more intense experience walking west of Dingle. Apart from the fact that the culture is different, this being a gaelic-speaking area, the scenery is much more rugged and history seems to invest the very landscape.

From Dingle town (44 01), travel west — either along the seafront or past the hospital — onto the Slea Head road by crossing Milltown bridge. Your view across the harbour is of Eask Hill with its fingerpost tower and beneath it the woods of Burnham enclosing the former residence of Lord Ventry, now an Irish-speaking college for girls, *Colaiste Ide*. Travel uphill straight through the crossroads. As you approach the crest of the hill, opposite the graveyard is a standing stone oddly juxtapositioned with a pseudo-Georgian house. This is part of a complex of two standing stones, a pair known locally as *Geatai na Gloire* (Gates of Paradise) — the remains of a megalithic tomb — and a boulder decorated with rock art.

Just over the hill, go off the Slea Head/Ventry road by continuing straight onto a byroad, bordered with fuchsia, honeysuckle and blackberry. Once again, uphill through a crossroads onto a road now bordered in season with the rich orange flower, montbretia. The profusion of flower and hedgerow in West Kerry is encouraged by the temperate climate. There is a second slight ascent on the surfaced road before you go right (beside the house with the red-tile roof after the 'Slow. Children Crossing' sign) onto another surfaced byroad. About 400m/yds on, watch for a green road on the left. As you travel, you will find this is genuinely green with fern, rushes, foxglove, thistle and nettle — you may need to cover up if in shorts! Continue northwest up *Bothar a' Chinn* (Road of the Head). The high stone walls, well mossed and covered in plant life, restrict views but as you approach the top before turning west, a lower fenceline allows views right of Dingle and, stretching north, the Brandon Ridge. At the crest, Rathinnane castle comes into view. The line of *Bothar a' Chinn* continues past the castle onto Ballyferriter but your course ahead will be along the coast to the south of Croaghmarhin (behind the castle) and Mount Eagle (to its left). Leaving the saddle, go right across a stone stile by a wire and fishing-net fence and, still on green road, swing left to gain your first glimpse of Ventry strand.

As you continue, you meet a gate; keep straight on over unsurfaced road. 60m/yds west of the gate, set in the stone wall on the left of the road, is a cross-inscribed slab. In the field to the south is an Early Christian church site, Kilcolman (*Cill na gColman*). If you have not seen ogham writing, search out a large boulder with two inscribed crosses. The writing consists of strokes along a stem line up the left side of the face and across the top, interpreted as (translation) 'My name is Colman, pilgrim' thus giving the site its name.

As you walk west, the full extent of Ventry harbour comes into view and 0.75km/0.4miles from the gate, just as the descent begins and the ruin of Rathinnane castle again becomes visible, watch for a green road on the left, with plenty of evidence of daily use by cows, which will take you onto surfaced road and directly to the harbour. (Before entering the green road, you may consider continuing a few metres/yards west to view the neat sheep gate built into the stone fence on the right.) At the crossroads, the village is on the left and the Way continues onto the beach straight ahead. I recommend going right, to the Bradan Feasa Café for refreshment. You can also invest in pottery and educate yourself in the myths of Ireland through the murals and, if possible, have a chat with the owner, Maurice Sheehy, who as well as being one of the developers of the Dingle Way is also a writer of guidebooks.

You are at the location of the Battle of Ventry, fought between the Fianna, Ireland's legendary standing army on one side and the fleets of the King of Spain and the King of the World on the other. It lasted a year and a day with massive losses on both sides. Go west along the beach across two streams and leave it before the loop to the pier for a sandy track leading to surfaced road where you go straight/leftish and then right at a T-junction into a cluster of houses, right again at the next T to end at a farmyard and house with neat fuchsia hedge at Caheratrant. To the right of the house is a green road which travels northwest before swinging to loop west between narrow walls. You can understand how in winter or even on a clear summer night it deserved the name *Bothar Dorcha* (Dark Road). This was the route to the school at Kilvickadownig, clearly seen as you emerge.

Just before the school, you meet the Slea Head road again. Go left and almost immediately, cross the road to enter a short stretch of green road beginning between the gables of two bungalows. Go through a gate and at the end of the road, cross a stile, go straight across the field and over a stone fence to regain the green road. The Way now continues west more or less parallel to, but above, the motor road, giving you even better views than those the coach passengers must pay for. It is said that this area has the greatest concentration of archaeological remains in Ireland and with little detour you will be able to sample two. Descend through fuchsia bushes to Fahan village onto a short stretch of surfaced road which can be used for access to Dunbeg (*Dun Beag*, Small Fort), which is below on the left across the main road. Excavation of the promontory fort suggested habitation from 550 BC to the tenth or eleventh century AD.

Leave the surfaced road after 150m/yds or so to go right onto green road, meeting the first of the specially designed tubular steel pole stiles. Bearing left to follow the clear path west on the hill side of the stone wall, ascend to the saddle and pause for the views — behind is all of Dingle Bay and the Brandon Ridge; ahead, the Atlantic with one of the Blasket Islands (west) and the Skellig Rock (southwest). Approaching Glenfahan

Stream, bear left again over another stile and descend right on a narrow track (stream in winter?) to the bridge. It is interesting to note that while there is a bridge here on the byroad, below the Glenfahan Stream crosses the main road on cobblestones, familiar to fans of car advertisements on TV. Across the stream, go left of old dwellings and keep a keen eye for *clochans*/beehive huts under the path, well covered with vegetation, one of which you can enter. Resume contouring west at the upper side of the stone fence with steel stiles confirming the route. Shortly, the second Blasket Island comes into view and as the third appears, you are rounding Slea Head and are in 'the nearest parish to America'. After the last steel pole stile, you can descend through fields aiming for the car park but remembering that there are cliffs on your left. The cliffs of Coumeenoole are in view beyond, decorated unfortunately by the wreckage of the *Ranga*, a Spanish ship washed up in a storm some years ago. Through the gate, you have the choice of going left to make a visit to Slea Head with its Calvary grotto or going right to Dunquin. If you have been lucky enough to reserve accommodation at Dunquin, I recommend an overnight stop here but if you are hostelling, you will have to continue a few more kilometres/miles north — see Walk 45.

As marking at this point is scarce as I write, if you are travelling the Way in reverse, go through the gate and bear right uphill by the stone wall to meet the first steel pole stile and marker.

Distance: 22km/14miles. Ascent: 365m/1,200ft. Walking time: 6½ hours.

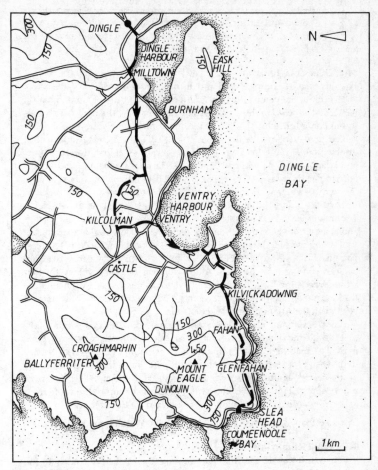

Reference OS Map: Sheet 20 (1:126,720).

44. CROAGHMARHIN/MOUNT EAGLE

Sliabh an Fhiolair, Mount Eagle (517m/1,696ft) is the western-most peak in the Dingle Peninsula. It provides very pleasant walking but arrangements may have to be made for transport at each end.

44(a) Over Croaghmarhin

For the sake of completeness and in order to gain views of the north and south of the peninsula, I prefer to include the peak of Croaghmarhin (*Cruach Mharthain*) in this walk. At Ballyferriter, take the road which goes uphill behind the church (355 043). Almost immediately, beyond the flat-roofed house, follow the first fence (right) uphill and swing right with it up the point of the spur. There is an obvious line — at first, upright stones, and later, a fence. As you rise, Smerwick Harbour lies behind and Ventry Harbour is on your left. Northwest is Sybil Point and on this side of it, Ferriter's Cove, famous for the fossils which can be seen on the rocks. In front of the beach, the cluster of white buildings is the Dun an Oir Hotel. The architect is to be complimented on the design — a few walls and bushes and at least from here, the fiction of a traditional village would be complete.

Having reached the summit (405m/1,331ft), *Speicin Mharthain*, I suggest you go a little west to inspect points of interest. Directly ahead, a road can be seen coming into the bogs. Along this was built the village for that bitter-sweet film *Ryan's Daughter*. Beyond is the jagged Minnaunmore Rock, made of fused volcanic fragments. To the southwest is Dunquin, and beyond, in the Atlantic, the Blasket Islands.

Look south and Mount Eagle rises before you. Descend south-south-east (beside the line of a fence) for the saddle fitted with communications mast. The road here is an escape route to Dunquin to the west or Ventry to the east. From the saddle, continue with the line of the fence (could this be the parish boundary?) to Coumaleague Hill (245m/800ft) and over point 340m/1,116ft to meet the turf cuttings at the top of the route from Kildurrihy. You can now follow the second part of the alternative walk.

Distance: 9km/5.5miles. Ascent: 700m/2,300ft. Walking time: 4 hours.

44(b) From Kildurrihy

If you wish to avoid the first summit, take the road from Ventry to the village of Kildurrihy (353 001). Continue on the road towards the corrie lake, *Loch Chill Uru* (Mount Eagle Lake on the map). The lake is a pleasant place to sit. Unlike most coombes, there are no overpowering rock walls — rock at the back but gradual gorse and heather clad slopes at each side. Swans make their home here in summer and you may also find the place alive with rabbits. Turn again from the lake to the green road which gently zig-zags to the saddle above where there has been much turf-cutting, some recent. The green road continues south a good part of the way to the cairned summit of Mount Eagle from where you have splendid views.

If you have decided on a horseshoe around the lake, pick your route down with care — it might be better to return as you came.

We will continue south-southwest, over the rocky shoulder of Beenacouma (425m/1,395ft) and directly ahead for Slea Head. Keeping the Blasket Island on your right and Skelligs Rock in view directly ahead, you pass many stone sheep shelters on the way. Just after the shoulder, you meet a square mesh wire fence. The steeper ground is avoided either by keeping east (left) of the fence until you cross it where the surfaced road below can be seen or keeping west (right) to descend to the Slea Head car park which is to the north of the actual Head.

Distance: 5km/3miles. Ascent: 500m/1,600 ft. Walking time: 2½ hours.

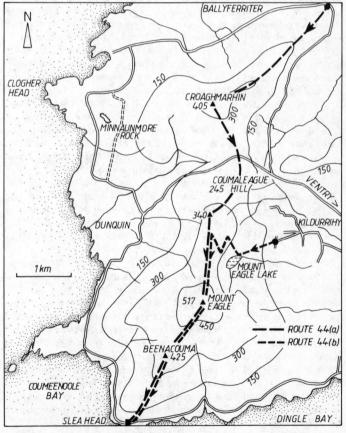

Reference OS Map: Sheet 20 (1:126,720).

45. (DINGLE WAY 5) SLEA HEAD-FEOHANAGH

The next leg of the Dingle Way takes us north along the Atlantic cliffs before turning east to begin the return journey. For those interested, there are three localities in close proximity at the start of the walk, which are described in Ralph Horne's Dingle Geological Guide — *Slea Head, Coumeenoole and Dunquin Harbour.*

From the Slea Head car park where Walk 43 ended (316 974), walk 2.5km/1.5miles north past Coumeenoole strand. As the road rises, you will see ahead the zig-zag path down to Dunquin pier, from where a ferry can be taken to the Blasket Islands. With the descent, the bay becomes clearer as does the multi-coloured layering on the sea cliffs which despite their sheerness are well covered with growth. At the Y-junction, take the left fork over the cliffs and left again onto unsurfaced road. This shortly becomes green road passing a line of partly-restored stone houses, and swings left over the stream running down to Cusheen (*Cuaisin*, Little Inlet). Many of the beaches at this end of the peninsula have dangerous currents and I would not recommend bathing here (or at Clogher beach which we meet later). Cross the stream at the stony beach and go right up the road past the sheep-dipping tank.

To the left of the road is the site proposed for the Blasket Islands Interpretative Centre. The project is an exciting one covering the literature and history of the islands as well as providing archives for students. The plans show a strong and dramatic building and, as I write, there is a certain amount of agonising in relation to both the design and the siting. By the time you pass, you may be able to judge for yourself.

One km/0.5miles or so later you reach the Youth Hostel at a crossroads. Go straight through and continue uphill (if you are interested in paintings, a sign marks the studio of Maria Simmonds-Gooding on the left) to a Y-junction just before the surfaced road ends. The right fork leads to the former location of the village constructed for the film *Ryan's Daughter* which did so much to publicise the scenery of Dingle.

Your course is left over a small concrete bridge and immediately right as a Way marker directs you onto what seems open bog. However, two raised banks confirm that this was the line of an old road and this becomes more definite as you push north to the saddle where you get your first view of The Three Sisters headland. Minnaunmore Rock on the left of the saddle is one of the few examples of volcanic activity in Ireland, consisting of welded fragments of lava (locality 10 in Ralph Horne's book). Descend to the surfaced road at Graigue, go right past another studio, this time that of a potter, Louis Mulcahy. 20m/yds or so beyond *Potadoireacht na Caoloige*, watch for the surfaced road left which leads to a path past (or through) another sheep-dipping tank down to the beach at Clogher — heed the earlier warning about bathing and be content with a break for lunch.

Go right up the access road to meet the main road, go straight and left almost immediately onto an unsurfaced road (marked 'shore angling'). The sea-stacks in view ahead are an indication of the cliffs over which you will travel — care may be needed if travelling on a stormy day but in fine weather, the contrast of rock and water, profuse vegetation and wild birds will enrich your journey. Follow the road as it peters out and becomes first a double line made by tractor tyres and later the single line of a sheeptrack through fields. Approaching Ballincolla (*Baile an Chalaidh*, Town of the Harbour, still provides berthage for fishing boats), you will see on your right the backs of two cottages. Beginning as two deeply-gouged tractor-tyre marks in the field, the Way emerges through a field gate to the left of the cottages. Onto the surfaced road, take the second turn left through the hamlet, skirting the bay until you reach Dun an Oir golf course and hotel. If you have time for a detour, there is much of interest nearby — a promontory fort with fifteenth/sixteenth-century tower-house, Ferriter's Castle; shell middens on the cliff-face; fossils, lava flow and other geological features well described by Ralph Horne.

Go right on a track beside the last chalet in the hotel complex and follow the path skirting the northern edge of the golf course to join sur-faced road again at Ballyoughteragh (*Baile Uachtarach*, Upper Town). Follow this road for 2km/1.2miles, keeping left at the first junction to pass a greenhouse complex protected by a log palisade. Reaching a T-junction, go right, aiming for the beach at Smerwick Harbour. The name is thought to be of norse origin from *smoer* (butter) and *wick* (harbour). A detour to the left will take you to Castel del Oro (*Dun an Oir*, Fort of Gold), a promontory fortified by seven or eight hundred Spaniards who came in a fleet of six ships in 1580 to support the Desmond Rebellion. While the fort was well armed (4 gun emplacements and arms and ammunition for 4,000 men) and stocked (provisions for 6 months), the garrison surrendered after three days' siege. The occupants were all beheaded by the English army in a nearby field known as *Gort na Gearradh* (Field of the Cutting), their corpses thrown in the sea and their heads buried in fields known as *Gort na gCeann* (Field of Heads). The poet, Edmund Spenser, was on the English side. Today, the promontory is peaceful but its isolated position shows how easily it was surrounded and besieged from land and sea.

The Way continues along *Beal Ban* (White Strand) over two streams with views northeast to Ballydavid Head and east of it Masatiompan, both features on the next leg of the Way. At Wine Strand, which may be another reference to Spanish aid, join the road briefly through the village/chalet development to avoid the rough rocks at Carrigveen/Ballinrannig point — unless your enthusiasm for geology obliges you to visit another of Ralph Horne's localities. The *gallan* (standing stone) crowning a large grass-grown sandy knoll is the single remaining example of seven ogham stones, all others being removed elsewhere in the last century. Keeping left, with the square ruin of the fifteenth-century Fitzgerald Castle in sight ahead, return to the beach, crossing the stream by stepping-stones. You are now close to Gallarus Oratory, the only example left in Ireland of a stone 'boat-shaped' church, worth a visit if you are prepared to make a detour of 2.5km/1.5miles. Beyond the gaelic football pitch enclosed with wire fence, go right onto the road to Murreagh village (*An Mhuirioch*, Sandy Soil) — refreshments available at the shop. Take the road left, past the post office on the right with the mast of *Raidio na Gaeltachta* in sight ahead. You are now approaching *Baile na nGall* (Town of the Foreigners) which has laboured under two names since the Ballydavid coastguard station was moved west to this point.

Go left to the pier, where there is a public house (with food) and registered hostel. At the pier, go right and onto a track leading north from the houses between stone walls to the cliff edge. A short distance along, you meet a watch hut built during the period known in Ireland as the Emergency and known elsewhere as World War II. A clear sheep track leads along the cliff tops, rich in plant and bird life. It is hardly necessary to say take care not to approach too close to the cliff edge. Sheltering behind the stone wall from biting rain borne by northeasterly winds straight from Iceland, I disturbed a fulmar, a bird extremely rare early this century but now a common summer visitor on all coasts. Over the saddle, you join the road by the round house. To the right of it is a café but if not in need of rest, go left passing Dooneen pier on the left (road closed 1990 due to storm damage) downhill to Feohanagh where a public house offers welcome respite.

Distance: 23km/12miles. Ascent: 215m/700ft. Walking time: 6¼ hours.

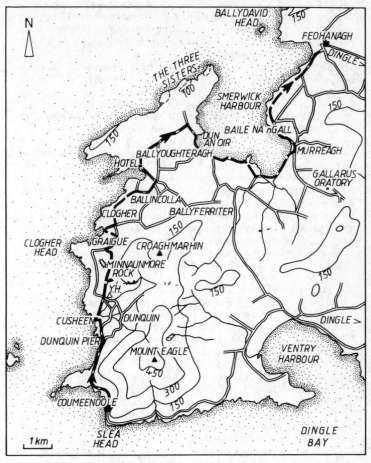

N

BALLYDAVID HEAD
150
FEOHANAGH
DINGLE
THE THREE SISTERS
100
SMERWICK HARBOUR
150
BAILE NA nGALL
DUN AN OIR
BALLYOUGHTERAGH
150
MURREAGH
HOTEL
GALLARUS ORATORY
BALLINCOLLA
CLOGHER
BALLYFERRITER
GRAIGUE
150
CLOGHER HEAD
CROAGHMARHIN
MINNAUNMORE ROCK
Y.H.
150
150
CUSHEEN
DUNQUIN
DINGLE
DUNQUIN PIER
MOUNT EAGLE
450
VENTRY HARBOUR
300
COUMEENOOLE
150
SLEA HEAD
DINGLE BAY

1 km

Reference OS Map: Sheet 20 (1:126,720).

46. MOUNT BRANDON

Outside of the MacGillycuddy's Reeks, Mount Brandon at 953m/3,127ft is the country's highest peak and, in many ways, it is the finest climb. There are rewards for the lover of scenery, for the geologist and for the botanist, and the mountain deserves repeated visits.

There are two routes — a gradual one from the west and the much more spectacular one from the east — and I have combined both, leaving you to adjust as you see fit. Given the opportunity, the eastern approach (from Faha, a townland on the slope above Cloghane village) is without doubt the better. Follow the signposts from Cloghane and park your car above the severe S-bend at the upper end of the surfaced road (494 118) near Miss O'Connor's house. There is a telephone here and it would be wise to leave a note on your windscreen (route and expected time of arrival) in case of an emergency. Here, a further signpost directs you to a grotto from which a line of poles leads along the shoulder. These were erected to guide those taking part in the pilgrimage to the oratory above. As you contour along below the skyline, you are walking under the site of a number of aircraft crashes. These occurred in the early days of flying, and wreckage can still be seen if you care to detour. The wrecks include one of a German fighter plane which belly-landed and exploded in 1940.

During the traverse of the shoulder, a perfectly shaped peak stands ahead — this is Brandon Peak. The boulder field descending to a wide scree field is known locally as *Gran Ceol* — Grain Music or Ugly Music: the 'music' is created as rocks tumble during a storm.

It is when you reach the turning point at the *Tobar* (a spring well — a welcome amenity if your trip is on a hot day) that the interest really begins. You now sit over Lough Cruttia (*Loch Cruite*, Harp Lake) and Lough Nalacken (*Loch na Lacha*, Duck Lake) and these in their rock setting give a hint of what is to come. The path now continues northwest in the side of the narrow ice-carved glen. Any description of mine would fail to do justice to the geological grandeur created by the scree slopes and the sheer walls, their curved rock layers laid bare for our inspection, towering above the line of paternoster lakes. The *Dingle Geological Guide* gives all the technical data.

For the botanist, there are equal pleasures. Already, the insectiverous butterwort (plentiful) and sundew (less in evidence) were to be seen along the slope above Faha. Now, St Patrick's cabbage can be seen among the rocks by the path and the primitive club moss is to be found by the inner lakes. But it is at the end of the valley inside the two last small lakes that the rarest alpine flora (survivors on uncovered peaks during the Ice Age) are to be found — just to the left of the path as it commences to rise up the esk. Each plant may be found in one or two other areas in these islands but it is only in Brandon that all are to be seen in close proximity.

My first incursion here was in snow and these seemed ideal conditions to appreciate what the Ice Age had created. It also led to another experience — the smell of a fox who had just passed by and had left fresh pad marks on the snow at the bottom of the esk. The smell (like burning rubber is the best description I can give) was still there on our return an hour or so later.

Beyond the lakes, the path swings (right) up the esk/steep gully to take you to the saddle north of the peak. This is a good spot to look back and see how the lakes beside which you travelled have been trapped on rock shelves. Here, the western end of the Dingle Peninsula and the Blasket Islands lie before you and you can also look down on the perfect amphitheatre of Maughanveel to the northeast.

A short rise of 90m/300ft or so (now over an almost sheer drop of 300m/1,000ft — please be careful) takes you to the summit marked by the remains of *Teampaillin Breanainn*/St Brendan's Oratory, another rectangular building and a holy well. No date has been put on the constructions but it is suggested that building lasted over 1,400 years. St Brendan (the Navigator) is supposed to have reflected here before setting out with a band of fellow-monks in a frail curragh on their journey to Greenland and America. *Sliabh Daidche* was the peak's name in pre-Christian times and it was apparently the site of a Celtic harvest celebration. If there are views (Brandon is termed a wet mountain and generally has a cloud sitting on its summit), these are understandably magnificent — sea, land, rock and lake.

From the peak you may decide to retrace your steps — take care on the esk. Alternatively, you can descend in a south-westerly direction roughly on the line of the Saints Road. Care should be taken leaving the top — the western side is rounded and the lie of the land may pull you into the coombes on either side. Keep to the centre of the shoulder. The boggy top changes to a steeper rockier section before levelling off again to bog, marked with a few standing stones. A path is now somewhat discernible and it runs down to the right of a deep-cut stream (a dried-up stream bed at times) and finally crosses it to meet the stony bohereen which leads to Ballybrack.

While this is a favourite haunt, I must record a few complaints. The markers on the early part of the path are of dubious value, merely encouraging those better-off on low-level routes. The whitewashing brush used to paint the rocks along the pilgrim's route may, I think, have been applied too liberally. On the summit, the tubular steel cross looks obscene — a small stone plaque would be much more appropriate. Lastly, a doubt rather than a complaint, the new plantation to the north of Lough Cruttia may not be an improvement from the visual point of view. One could argue that trees once covered this entire area and there is also the question of employment provided. However, particularly when looking from the Conair Pass road beside the perfect coombe of Lough Doon (the Pedlar's Lake) where the effects of Ice Age glaciation were first recognised in Ireland, the barrenness emphasises the scouring and carving effects of the ice. But these are small matters — nature has worked on such a grand scale that man's puny efforts have little effect. Mount Brandon still remains one of my favourite climbs.

Distance: 7.5km/4.5miles. Ascent: 780m/2,550ft. Walking time: 4–5 hours.

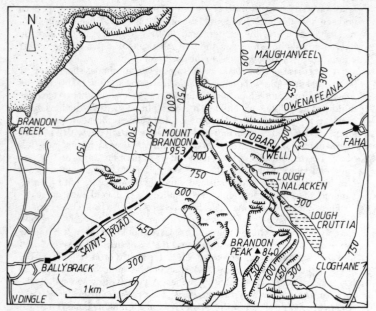

Reference OS Map: Sheet 20 (1:126,720).

↑

It has been the practice to travel south-north when doing the ridge, making use of the height gained by starting at the car park at the top of the Conair Pass. However, feeling that the views are better when walking in the opposite direction, this is the description I give. This option is made easier now by the improved bog road leading to Arraglen.

From Brandon village, simply follow the yellow Dingle Way markers leading west past the south gable of O'Neill's shop and along the bog road, which saves 4km/2.5miles walking and about 300m/1,000ft of climb. Don't forget to close all gates. If you are parking, do so with consideration. The road is used for transporting peat from the bogs and by farmers tending sheep. If your party is large, it would be selfish to leave a number of vehicles here and you should arrange to have them taken to your finishing point. Arraglen (480 150) is now a ruined village abandoned in the 1870s. The last child to walk to school in Brandon from here died in 1950 aged 80. Through the gap, one can see the coast of Clare. Local weatherlore tells that it is a sign of bad weather if you can see the Loop Head lighthouse, while good conditions hide it in a haze. The clifftops of Sauce Creek are obvious to the east.

From the end of the bog road, the yellow arrows lead west-southwest to the saddle south of Masatiompan mountain, said to derive its name from *tympanum* (drum). On the saddle is an ogham stone, marked 'monument' on OS maps. In the past century, the stone has fallen twice and on one occasion became buried. As I write, it stands as if to guard the pass. Both faces of the stone bear Maltese crosses and the ogham inscription (along both edges and across the top) reads in translation: Ronan the priest son of Comgan.

The ridge goes southwest from the stone. Some 200m/yds from it is a heap of stones. Locals say that it is the remains of a signal tower built in the early nineteenth century but not used because of persistent mist. The military road approaching the saddle from the west (Walk 48) supports this theory. Continue over two rock outcrops and onto boggy ridge. The rock walls Maghanveel, of the Owenafeana River valley, are typical of the Brandon area. It is not necessary to take in the next summit, unless you insist on 'bagging' all, and you can contour along the western flank to arrive at the top of the esk where you join the path from Faha and continue to the top of Mount Brandon (see Walk 46 for further information).

Descending from Mount Brandon, the route now follows a perfectly visible stone wall which goes southeast and south virtually the whole way to Brandon Peak (840m/2,764ft). Approaching the Peak, left below you is Lough Cruttia with the boulder fields (*Gran Ceol*) running into it. As I write, the first wire sheep fence on the ridge is met just before the Peak. You could contour once again to the west but it would be a pity to miss the opportunity of sitting on the top and admiring the view. On a fine summer day, the blue waters of Brandon Bay with the lush vegetation at Fermoyle sweeping down to an almost white beach take on a Caribbean look. To the southeast are the MacGillycuddy's Reeks and you are looking directly into Coomloughra enclosed by part of the highest ridge walk in Ireland. The Blasket Islands and Skellig Rock stand in the Atlantic to the west and southwest. It is encouraging also to look behind you at this stage and appreciate how far you have travelled. The summit of the Peak consists of a mini-arête and after it, you meet the second wire fence, considerably provided with a gate. Lough Doon is directly in view across the Conair Pass road. The ridge now swings southwest to descend to a boggy plateau which suffers from wind erosion. The tracks of tractor wheels are visible and if the weather or time dictates, there is a farm road offering an escape route east into Mullaghveal valley. Approaching the saddle, keep to the right of the wire fence by using (and closing) the gate. An old road, not visible on the saddle but quite clear lower down, connected Mullaghveal and Glin North, well serviced by bog roads to the west. This gives another escape route and if you had studied your map in advance, you might have decided on having transport here for a pick-up.

We will continue over the summit named Ballysitteragh on the OS map (625m/2,050ft). During the ascent, the lakes in Mullaghveal, five below you and one behind, come gradually into view, the names of two — Lough Gal (*Loch Geal*, Bright Lake) and Lough Duff (*Loch Dubh*, Black Lake) — reflecting the light in this narrow coombe. Once over the summit, you will see the mouth of Dingle Harbour. The inner harbour and the town gradually come into view and the panorama of Iveragh Peninsula should spur you east over the soft ground across the few slight rises of Beennabrack (*Beanna Breac*, Speckled Peaks) and Beenduff (*Beann Dubh*, Black Peak). The peaks stand over the walls of Mullaghveal and you might pause for the view down before completing a course almost parallel with the road rising from Dingle to the car park at the top of the Conair Pass (490 055).

Distance: from Arraglen 14.5km/9miles. Ascent: 1,450m/4,750ft. Walking time: 7–8 hours.

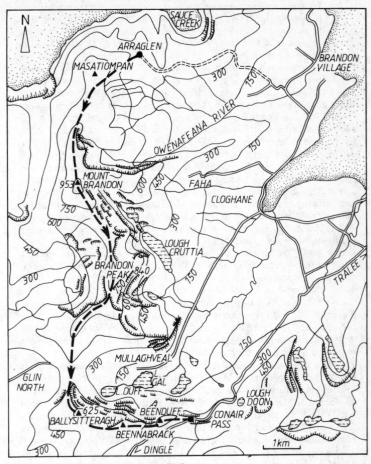

Reference OS Map: Sheet 20 (1:126,720).

48. (DINGLE WAY 6) FEOHANAGH-CLOGHANE

The next leg of the Dingle Way takes you onto the highest ground on the route, close enough to 700m/2,250ft, an area subject to mist and you should be careful that both the weather and you are fit for it. You will be rewarded with splendid views.

Leave Feohanagh (39 09) on a northerly course across the bridge and uphill to a T-junction. Go right to travel east under another World War II watch hut on craggy Ballydavid Head, with the cliffs over Brandon Creek coming into view. Stay right with the surfaced road at the Y, then straight through the crossroads (right is an escape route to Dingle) and left to the end of surfaced road at Tiduff (*Tir Dubh*, Black Country). West is Brandon Creek, from where legend says St Brendan set sail in his fragile craft to discover America centuries before Christopher Columbus, a feat repeated by the explorer/writer Tim Severin in recent years. Off the surfaced road, go right through a gate. The green road to the saddle can be seen and to gain it, you should depart (right) from the mountain road inside the gate and remain close to the wire fence. Gradually, the built-up form of the military road will become clearer and as you reach the first saddle, you will be pleasantly surprised to find that you are half-way to the main saddle. Beennaman to your left is described in the *Dingle Geological Guide*. To the east of it and north of your line of travel is a steep valley running down to the sea known to locals as 'the green fields', otherwise Foherna-managh (*Fothair na Manach*, Deep Glen of the Monks). St Brendan is said to have established a monastery on this site, chosen no doubt for its isolation. You will see field walls below by carefully picking your steps to the edge, but a descent and return would be outside the range of the average walker. The Archaeological Survey report does not contain details of any finds, stating that the ecclesiastical nature of the settlement is suggested only by the name and folklore.

While the military road is at times less clear (absorbed into the bog) as you ascend further on the Way, you should have no trouble staying on course east until you arrive beside the ogham stone/monument on the saddle below Masatiompan and the ruins of the signal tower to the west (see Walk 47 for description). Take a last look west at The Three Sisters and Ballydavid Head before taking in the view east — the sweep of Brandon Bay, the Magharees and Tralee Bay by which you will travel if continuing on the Way. From the saddle follow the marked course east downhill, the reverse of the ascent in Walk 47, through Arraglen and with sight of the safe haven of Brandon pier encouraging you on, down the bog road to reach the gable end of O'Neill's shop.

(If you are on a return trip from the west and you have the appetite, a circular tour can be achieved by picking steps carefully along the more precipitous route from Arraglen, contouring well above the steep cliffs of Sauce Creek and then south of Bookeen to the car park on Brandon Head. I would not recommend this unless you are sure of your navigation.)

At the shop, go left on the surfaced road and left again, still on surfaced road, to loop clockwise down to meet a T-junction, where you go right for Brandon village. Farran ringfort, now much overgrown, is in a field left of the road approaching the junction. It features in a folktale of the locality which tells of crying, heard on the death of an infant, travelling through the townland and dying away only on entering the fort. You may wish to pause for refreshment in the village or detour to the pier to view the fishing boats or buy fish. Continue to the post office and go behind it to the footbridge across the Owennafeana River. Go left through the small gate at the end of the footbridge and 20m/yds along the beach to meet tractor tyre tracks and exit at a gate to surfaced road serving beachgoers. Keep straight/rightish and travel through Ballyquin to rejoin the road from Brandon village to Cloghane. Over the crest of the road with view ahead of the inlet, turn right at the crossroads to follow the signs for *Cnoc Breanainn*/Brandon Mountain. The next leg of the marked route could be very wet in winter and if your footwear is unsuitable, you have the choice of continuing through the crossroads to Cloghane. Assuming you are remaining on the Way, your journey is 2km/1.25miles uphill on surfaced road, disregarding surfaced roads left and right — although after 0.5km/0.3miles, you could detour right onto a byroad to reach the Cloonsharragh stone alignment, orientated on the rising sun at the summer solstice but claimed by locals to be the headstones of kings. Travelling uphill, the village of Cloghane and church ruin are in view below on the left before you meet the turnoff. Reaching the two-storey house on the right, you hear a stream and can enter left just beyond it — don't be deterred by the overgrown entrance. Go right immediately, through the small gate, and travel downhill with the wire fence on your left until you meet a gap in the fence and stepping-stones leading back over the stream. Follow the muddy path down to and left along by the river, cross at the footbridge and, keeping the church tower in view, go through the fields to *Bothar an Teampaill* (Road of the Church). (Incidentally, if you are travelling the Way in reverse from Cloghane, take the first gate right after the gate left into the churchyard — don't follow the green road, unless of course a change of route has been clearly marked.) The ruins of the thirteenth century church are worth a visit if only to view the unexpected pagan relic. At eye-level, projecting from the internal southern wall, is the face of the Celtic harvest god, Crom Dubh.

Cloghane is well endowed with hostelries although if you are in need of overnight accommodation, it is best to have booked in advance.

Distance: 28km/17.5miles. Ascent: 790m/2,600ft. Walking time: 9 hours.

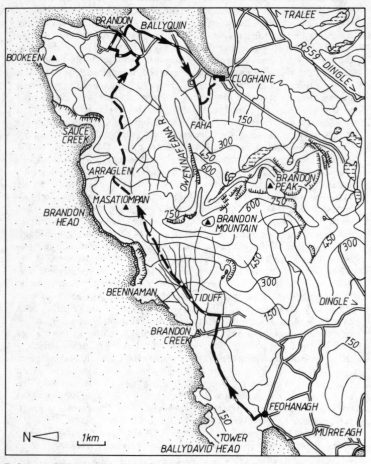

Reference OS Map: Sheet 20 (1:126,720).

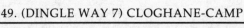

The nature of the Way now changes radically, much being along beach.
Unless intending to travel this leg in full, you should consider in
advance transport and accommodation or be prepared to take a short cut.

From Cloghane village (51 11), travel south and east, skirting the inner
end of Brandon Bay, a distance of just over 5km/3.25miles to Fermoyle.
On the leg east, you can enjoy another lesson *a la* Ralph Horne if armed
with his *Geological Guide*. Look south to Slievenalecka and Slievenagower
mountains with their north-facing corries and arêtes. After the two hump-
back bridges over the Scorid and Glenahoo rivers, opposite Fermoyle
House, a road leads to the beach on which you can remain for 10km/
6miles or so as far as Fahamore. I should mention that there are two
streams near the start and if there has been heavy rainfall on the hills
above, these may be swollen. In that event, you could continue on the road
to Stradbally allowing you to visit, on the way back to the beach, the well-
preserved remains of the late fifteenth/early sixteenth-century Strad-bally
church which has a nice window and other details. (If you are pressed for
time, Stradbally church connects by road direct to Castlegregory on an old
route from the west to Tralee.) Back on the beach, Lough Gill wildlife
sanctuary is just to the east. A golf course is being developed between it
and the sea and one cannot help questioning the wisdom of endangering
rare plants and fauna, this being one of the few habitats of the natterjack
toad. The entire peninsula is of interest, being a tombolo connecting the
upstanding limestone of the headland to the mainland — here again refer
to Ralph Horne's book. Travelling north and approaching Fahamore, a
glance west at Brandon Peak will confirm that you are now further north
than at any point so far. To avoid rocks underfoot, go right to join the road
and go left to the village. You could consider going back to the shore
opposite Spillane's public house and then right to inspect in the cliffs of
boulder clay a shell midden, refuse discarded by our ancestors, a practice
still honoured as you will have seen along the beach!

Fahamore still retains the flavour of a fishing village where occupants
also engage in agriculture. Go north on surfaced road, noting, as you swing
east for Scraggane Bay, evidence of the underlying rock in the new limestone wall. The few currachs, light frame boats originally covered with
hides but now made with canvas, still to be seen in the water, are used as
tenders for the fishing boats. It is difficult to believe that currachs were
once used to transport cattle to and from the Magharee Islands to the
north. The last family, Goodwins, left the islands in the early 1940s. On
the high point west of the pier, a black flag was flown if there was a
message for the islanders, and they raised a flag on the island in an
emergency.

The western shore of Scraggane Bay is rocky and as you swing south,
follow the path bordering the fields. Note the plots of carrots and other

vegetables, a reminder of the 1930s and 40s when the area was devoted to growing sugar beet and onions and *spailpíní* (migrant labourers) walked miles here for employment. Join the road at Candiha. The standing stone to the south is not worth the detour — the inscriptions are of recent origin. Continue around the bay to Kilshannig (*Cill Seanaigh*, Church of St Senach), another unspoilt village. The graveyard contains the church, possibly fifteenth/sixteenth century, built on an Early Christian foundation. An inscribed stone stands within the ruin. The tomb inside the gate is a Goodwin one. The family originally came to this area as watchtower keepers but the tower that stood at Kilshannig is in ruins.

Go south now, again along the beach — you have the option of taking a short cut to the road if easterly winds make travel unpleasant. On the beach, the view southwest is of Caherconree and, beneath it, Camp. The beach consists of three crescents, decreasing in size and, unless forced off by tide, continue until you meet the sign 'Dangerous Currents' where you must join the road to cross Trench Bridge, under which Lough Gill drains. Follow the road to Castlegregory village. Of the castle, all that remains are fragments in the garden at the rear of Egan's shop. You may remem-ber our visit to Minard Castle on an earlier stage of the Dingle Way. Castlegregory, also, was besieged by Cromwellian forces and the inhabi-tants fled for safety to Minard where they were 'blown up by powder'.

At the village, take the second left onto a laneway which continues through mudflats and becomes green road leading to a footbridge. Noting the Republican monument on the left, join a surfaced road past a beach and the Anchor Caravan Park, over a hump-back bridge and still straight to meet the Cloghane-Camp road just before the Tralee Bay Hotel. Leave it again after the hotel, opposite Aughacasla School, going left to the beach. At the beach, turn right and you can walk on the sandy shoreline for 4–5km/2.5–3miles, depending on where you decide to leave it. As is to be expected from the name (*Atha an Caisle*, Fords of the Sea-inlet), there are a number of streams, normally forded easily enough but you may be forced onto the Tralee-Dingle road if there has been a period of heavy rain or if the sea is particularly full or rough. Do not leave this too late as you soon meet sand cliffs topped with wire fence. After Carrigagharoe Point (*Carraigheacha Rua*, Red Crags), the low cliffs part to reveal a narrow laneway, on the left of which stands Kilgobbin church which had temporarily disappeared from view. The Anglican church was built in 1824, probably on an Early Christian site. By the north (side) door is a font base, the font itself bearing a 1729 inscription inside the building. The laneway can be used as an escape route to Camp in adverse tidal or river conditions. Return to the beach and continue on the Way, passing an exit on the right beside a concrete L-shaped wall and another just past the Finglas River of mythical fame. Some further distance along the shore, a group of pointed limestone rocks jutting from the sand alert you to watch for a marker. It is time to turn your back to the sea. Exit through a sandy cleft to a surfaced bohereen that leads to a T-junction on the R559/T68. (There are public-houses some 1.2km/0.75miles to the right at Castlegregory Junction — a spur of the Tralee & Dingle Light Railway to Castlegregory started here.) Turn left at the T-junction for 300m/yds (take care on a very busy road) and take a by-road right. This leads steeply for a few hundred metres/yards to join the outgoing Dingle Way by which you can retrace your steps, visiting Derrymore, Tonevane and Blennerville in the reverse direction.

If you are walking the route in reverse, the exit off the beach may not be clear. Pass the red cliffs of Carrigagharoe Point and go around a second set of red cliffs before finding the opening onto surfaced road near a small caravan park. If in doubt, the Tralee Bay Hotel is your reference point.

Distance: to Camp 37.5km/23miles. Ascent: 70m/250ft. Walking time: 9½ hours.

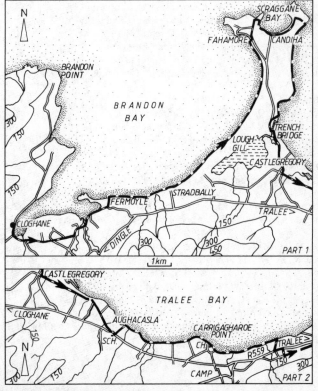

Reference OS Map: Sheet 20 (1:126,720).

General

Bellamy, Dr D., *The Wild Boglands*, Dublin 1986.

de Buitlear, E. (ed.), *Wild Ireland*, Dublin 1984.

Donaldson, F., *The Lusitanian Flora*, Dublin 1977.

Lynam, J. (ed.), *Irish Peaks*, London 1982.

Mitchell, F., *The Way that I Followed*, Dublin 1990.

Moriarty, C., *A Guide to Irish Birds*, Cork 1967.

Mulholland, H., *Guide to Eire's 3000-ft Mountains*, Birkenhead 1981.

National Library of Ireland, *Ireland from Maps*, Dublin 1980.

Nolan, W. (ed.), *The Shaping of Ireland*, Cork 1986.

Nolan, W., *Tracing the Past*, Dublin 1982.

O'Gorman, F. (ed.), *The Irish Wildlife Book*, Dublin 1979.

Perrott, D. and Lynam, J., *Walk Cork & Kerry*, Edinburgh 1990.

Pochin Mould, D.D.C., *The Mountains of Ireland*, Dublin 1976.

Praeger, R.L., *The Botanist in Ireland*, Dublin 1934.

Praeger, R.L., *The Way that I Went*, Dublin 1969.

Wall, C.W., *Mountaineering in Ireland*, Dublin 1976.

Whittow, J.B., *Geology and Scenery in Ireland*, Harmondsworth 1974.

Southwest

Barrington, T.J., *Discovering Kerry*, Dublin 1976.

Coleman, J.C., *The Mountains of Killarney*, Dundalk 1948.

Cuppage, J., *Archaeological Survey of the Dingle Peninsula*, Ballyferriter 1986.

Forest & Wildlife Service, *Gougane Barra Forest Park*, Dublin n.d.

Foley, K., *History of Killorglin*, Killorglin 1988.

Horne, R.R., *Geological Guide to the Dingle Peninsula*, Dublin 1976.

Kenmare Literary and Historical Society, *Kenmare Journal*, Kenmare 1982.

Killorglin History and Folklore Society, *Journal — Cois Leamhna*, Killorglin 1984.

MacMonagle, P., *Outbacks of Killarney*, Killarney 1988.

Mersey, R., *The Hills of Cork & Kerry*, Gloucester 1987.

Murphy, T., *Field Studies — Cappanalea OEC*, Killorglin 1987.

O Conchuir, D., *Chorca Dhuibhne Guide*, Ballyferriter 1977.

Sheehy, M., *The Dingle Peninsula — 15 Walks*, Dingle 1989.

Sheehy, M., *The Dingle Way and The Saints Road*, Dingle 1989.

The Warplane Research Group of Ireland, *The Last Flight of 43/30719*, Cork 1984.

*Glossary of the more common Irish words used in
Place Names*

Abha, abhainn (ow, owen) river
Achadh (agha, augh) field
Ail or *faill* cliff
Alt height or side of glen
Ard height, promontory
Ath ford

Baile (bally) town, townland
Bán (bawn, baun) white
Barr top
Beag (beg) small
Bealach (ballagh) pass
Beann (ben) peak or pointed mountain
Bearna (barna) gap
Bignian little peak
Bó cow
Bóthar (boher) road
Bothairin (bohereen) small (unsurfaced) road
Breac (brack) speckled
Brí (bree, bray) hill
Buaile (booley) summer dairy pasture
Buí yellow
Bun foot of anything, river mouth

Carn pile of stones
Carraig (carrick) a rock
Cathair (caher) stone fort
Ceann (ken) head, headland
Ceathramhadh (carrow, 'carhoo' at Dunquin) quarter of land
Ceapach plot of tillage ground
Cill cell, church
Clár plain, board
Cloch stone
Clochóg stepping-stones
Cluain (cloon) meadow (generally of a monastery, associated
    with early Christian sites)
Cnoc (knock, crock) hill
Coill (kyle, kill) wood
Coire cauldron, corrie
Cor rounded hill

Corrán (carraun)   sickle, serrated mountain
Cruach, cruachan   steep hill (rick)
Cúm (coum)   hollow, corrie

Dearg   red
Doire (derry)   oakgrove
Druim   ridge
Dubh (duff, doo)   black
Dún   fort, castle

Eas (ass)   waterfall
Eisc (esk)   steep, rocky gully

Fionn (fin)   white, clear
Fraoch (freagh)   heath, heather

Gabhar (gower)   goat
Gallan   standing stone
Gaoith (gwee)   wind
Glais   streamlet
Glas green
Glas loch   small mountain lake
Gleann (glen)   valley
Gort   tilled field

Inbhear (inver)   river mouth
Inis   island

Lágh (law)   hill
Leac   flagstone
Leaca, leachan (lackan)   side of a hill
Leacht   monument
Learg   side of a hill
Leitir (letter)   wet hillside
Liath (lea)   grey
Loch (lough)   lake or sea inlet
Lug, lag   hollow

Machaire (maghera)   plain
Mael, maol (mweel)   bald, bare hill
Maigh   plain
Mám, madhm (maum)   pass
Más   long, low hill
Mór (more)   big
Muing   long-grassed expanse
Mullach   summit

Oilean island

Poll hole, pond

Riabhach grey
Rinn headland
Rua, ruadh red

Scairbh (scarriff) shallow ford
Scealp rocky cleft
Sceilig (skellig) rock
Sceir (sker, pl. skerry) rock, reef (Norse)
Sean old
Sescenn (seskin) marsh
Sidh (shee) fairy, fairy hill
Sliabh (slieve) mountain
Slidhe (slee) road, track
Spinc, splinc pointed pinnacle
Srón nose, noselike mountain feature
Sruth, sruthair, sruthán stream
Stuaic (stook) pointed pinnacle
Suí, suidhe (see) seat

Taobh, taebh (tave) side, hillside
Teach house
Teampull church
Tír (teer) land, territory
Tobar well
Tor tower-like rock
Torc wild boar
Tulach little hill